RAISING THE PROFILE
Marketing the HR Function

David Clutterbuck, co-founder and chairman of The ITEM Group plc, a business communications company, is an international management writer and speaker. His previous management books include *Everyone Needs a Mentor* published by the IPM, *The Winning Streak, The Marketing Edge* and *The Decline and Rise of British Industry*.

Desmond Dearlove is a business journalist. Former European editor of the Tom Peters' newsletter *On Achieving Excellence*, he is business issues editor at The ITEM Group and writes regularly for *The Times*.

D1350664

RAISING THE PROFILE
Marketing the HR Function

David Clutterbuck and Desmond Dearlove
with research by Lynne Fordham

INSTITUTE OF PERSONNEL MANAGEMENT

First published in 1993

Phototypeset by Photoprint, Torquay, Devon
and printed in Great Britain
by the Cromwell Press, Broughton Gifford, Wiltshire

British Library Cataloguing in Publication Data

Clutterbuck, David
  Raising the Profile: Marketing the HR
  Function. – (Developing Skills Series)
  I. Title II. Dearlove, Desmond
  III. Series
  658.3

  ISBN 0–85292–526–3

INSTITUTE OF PERSONNEL MANAGEMENT
. IPM House, Camp Road, Wimbledon, London SW19 4UX
Tel: 081-946-9100   Fax: 081-946-2570
Registered office as above. Registered Charity No. 215797
A company limited by guarantee. Registered in England No. 198002

Contents

Introduction

There's a Catch-22 that applies to human resources (HR) management. It goes something like this: 'We'll let you have your say in strategy,' say the board, 'when you show us that you can handle strategic decisions.'

'But how can I do that,' says the HR director, 'when you don't give me the power to make any?'

The answer, we believe, is for HR practitioners to reach out and take that power. But to do so they will have to raise the profile of HR in the organisations in which they operate and establish the credentials of HR as a strategic resource.

No one says it's going to be easy. But there is an opportunity open to them today by which they can demonstrate their strategic effectiveness. That opportunity lies in the way they position the HR function in the internal marketplace. To take advantage of this opportunity, however, HR will have to change radically. Most important of all, its practitioners must find ways to articulate – in terms that are meaningful to senior management and other functions – the value they add to the business. This is something that in the past they have singularly failed to do. The question that HR practitioners must ask themselves is why?

At the very heart of the matter, we believe, is the issue of the cultural separation of HR from other functions. This is often compounded by geographical separation, ineffective internal communications and poor marketing to other departments. It is here, however, that the germ of the solution lies.

The challenge facing HR departments today is to find ways to end their isolation and to build closer relationships with internal customers. In short, they must learn to market themselves more effectively. Over time, this will enhance their standing and provide a platform to give them a greater say in the running of the business.

At the same time, with HR functions in public sector organisations already facing up to the threat from compulsory competitive tendering, and moves towards outsourcing non-core functions in the private sector too, the time has come to develop defensive marketing strategies to ensure that the concept of the internal HR function survives. To do so, HR practitioners must convince strategy decision makers not only of their value today, but of the value they will add in the future.

Raising the profile of HR within the organisation is not a strategy without risks, however. For one thing, by deliberately stepping into the limelight, HR will be laying itself open to criticism, and worse still, drawing attention to its shortcomings. It is possible to stick your head too far above the parapet. One personnel department we came across decided to produce a brochure to put a friendly human face on their department by including photographs of everybody who worked in personnel. When senior managers saw all these smiling, approachable people in the department their reaction was, 'My God, what a lot of personnel people we've got' and promptly started to weed them out.

At the same time, however, a number of factors mean that in the next few years HR will be uniquely placed to make a greater strategic contribution. For one thing, impending skills shortages and demographic changes – much discussed at the end of the 1980s but largely masked by the recession in the early 1990s – will increasingly come home to roost. For another, the move to truly people-based strategies will accelerate as companies recognise that such strategies are the best way to create sustainable competitive advantage in a rapidly changing world. In tomorrow's slimmed-down, knowledge-led corporate structures there will be far less room for passengers – every employee must contribute. It will be HR's job to assist line managers in ensuring they do so. For HR to miss this chance would be a tragedy both for the profession and for the competitiveness of European business in the future.

We are pleased to report that in some organisations progress has already been made in this direction. Where possible we have tried to support our arguments with case-study material showing what can be achieved by applying marketing principles to HR. The HR practitioners in these organisations have begun a journey that all HR practitioners will sooner or later have to make. It is a journey towards shaping their own vision of the role of HR in the future.

Today, the HR profession in the UK stands at a crossroads. It can remain isolated, elitist and inward-looking; or it can assimilate itself within client organisations as a driving force for change. The latter will only happen, however, if senior HR professionals are prepared to listen more closely to their customers and learn from each other, from other staff departments and from best practice globally.

This book discusses how to market HR internally to achieve an effective market positioning. In doing so, it brings into question the entire *raison d'être* of the HR function. Does it exist for operational reasons defined by its own rigid borders? Is it there to implement people strategies set by top management? Or does it exist solely to service its line managers, responding constantly to their shifting needs?

The only way to understand these issues is to explore them alongside internal clients and customers. To do so will require a greater commitment to standing in line managers' shoes; and it will demand the courage to experiment, to challenge sacred cows, and to expose mistakes by HR, recognising them as valuable learning opportunities for the organisation as a whole.

And the prize? For those HR departments that accept and meet the challenge, the opportunity to become a central driving force not just in implementing business objectives, but in shaping them; not just following patterns of change, but becoming the role model for coping with the innate ambiguities of modern business.

HR professionals will need all the help they can get. We believe this book provides, if not the answers, at the very least some of the questions they need to answer if they are to survive and thrive in the radically changed business environment of the twenty-first century.

Those HR departments which bury their heads in the sand put at risk their very survival. There is no guarantee that the current roles of HR will continue to justify supporting a separate function. Many chief executive officers (CEOs) are already asking questions such as: 'If we can put out payroll and other services to the bank; if we can deliver most training through external contractors; if line management is meant to take more responsibility for developing people; why do we need HR at all?'

In short, the time is fast approaching when sitting on the fence is no longer an option for HR practitioners (and for many that time has already arrived). They must make up their minds now whether they wish to be regarded as a core strategic resource, subject to the same sorts of rigorous performance criteria as other parts of the business; or as a support function, whose survival depends upon continuing to be regarded as an acceptable overhead. They cannot have it both ways.

Ultimately then, the question for HR practitioners is a simple one: should they continue to worry about putting their heads above the parapet in case they have them shot off, or should they have the courage of their convictions and pursue strategies aimed at winning the influence and respect they claim to deserve? To put it another way: HR – man or mouse?

This is not a book for mice.

The original research

The use of marketing techniques to alter its strategic positioning is not a new issue for the HR function. In some UK organisations HR has been moving in this direction since the early and mid-1980s. However, the Institute of Personnel Management (IPM) felt that much more needed to be understood about their experience – successes and failures – if HR practitioners more generally were to profit from what they had learned.

As a first step, the IPM commissioned The ITEM Group to conduct an exploratory research study to investigate supplier-customer relationships between the HR function and line management. The intention was to look at how and to what extent those concerned with directing and managing the HR function were developing systematic approaches to marketing the function within their organisations.

The resulting report in 1991[1] focused on defining the scope of the marketing task required by looking at line management expectations and perceptions of need. It also examined the HR applications of established marketing techniques, particularly in the areas of market research and customer service. The aim was to move towards establishing best practice guidelines through a clear understanding of the issues.

At that time there were isolated examples of what could be achieved by HR departments applying the principles of internal marketing. However, much of the case-study material was sketchy, too closely tied to the historical circumstances of a particular organisation to draw general lessons, or too fresh for its impact to be properly assessed. As a result, the task of identifying best practice was set aside.

In the two years since the original report was completed, the pace of change has if anything increased. So has the need to learn from best practice among HR practitioners. Many involved with HR, both in the United Kingdom and in the United States, now see the internal customer-supplier relationship as the key to unlocking the boardroom door.

This book examines the issues and looks at practical steps to enable HR to realise its true strategic potential.

In doing so it aims to demonstrate how you as HR practitioners can influence your organisation for the better. In particular:

- Develop a strategy that allows you to spend more time and resources working strategically, rather than fighting other people's fires.
- Manage your people as effectively and profitably as possible.
- Raise the profile of the HR function to enable it to become a key driver of competitive advantage.
- By acting as a 'guinea-pig' during periods of intense organisational learning, become a change leader in your organisation.
- Make use of marketing tools and techniques and develop

a marketing plan to 'sell' HR and the services it provides to key market segments in the organisation, including the chief executive, senior management and line managers.

For the sake of consistency we have generally preferred the term 'HR' to 'personnel'. Inevitably, exceptions occur in some places. Typically this is where a function in a particular organisation calls itself personnel, or where using 'HR' is inappropriate for other reasons.

PART I
The Marketing Challenge

1

Why Market HR?

Most HR practitioners would probably agree that it makes sense for them to let other parts of the business know about the contribution they make to the business. For one thing, they know that presenting a strong business case for what they do is the best way to ensure that they keep their jobs.

In principle, then, one might expect this book to be preaching to the converted. After all, since it is the best way to ensure a continuing market for HR services, marketing must be a 'good thing'. Why then bother to set out the arguments at all?

Well, for one thing, the idea of marketing does not sit comfortably with the role many HR professionals see for themselves. Quite simply, it is not part of the HR mindset. Perhaps it conjures up too many images from the 1980s of men in red braces and designer suits and women with tight skirts and shoulder pads. Or maybe it is just that at first sight the notion of marketing seems alien to the 'people' side of business. As a result, for whatever reasons, the simplicity of its message is often overlooked. We define that message as follows:

> *The true purpose of marketing is to ensure the most profitable fit between what customers want and the goods and services a supplier provides.*

Marketing principles and techniques are as relevant to internal markets as they are to external markets. They work on the simple assumption that as long as customers have needs, then fulfilling those needs has a value. Therefore those who meet customers' real needs can continue to command a price in the marketplace.

What this means (returning to the complexities of business life in the 1990s) is that HR practitioners can use marketing techniques to ensure that the services they provide meet the needs of their customers, be they line managers, top management or workers on the shopfloor. But for some reason, when faced with the concept of marketing HR, the initial reaction of many of its practitioners is one of puzzlement.

This reaction, however, is often followed by an enthusiastic acceptance that there may well be a great deal more they could do to sell the benefits of HR and the professionalism of the HR function. Many also agree that as a professional service, the role of the HR practitioner is increasingly one of internal consultant, and the measurement of performance as customer satisfaction (meaning the line managers paying the bill rather than customers such as training course participants sent home with happy sheets between their teeth) puts a whole new perspective on HR activities.

In other ways, too, marketing methodology has much to recommend it to the HR practitioner. For example, a typical product-marketing approach would normally start with customer research. Useful questions for HR practitioners to ask in conducting similar research include: What are line managers' basic objectives, both covert and overt? What keeps them awake at night? What HR initiatives might help them snore contentedly instead? Test marketing with a small group of friendly line managers helps ensure that you really have understood the customers' needs. Once this is done, you can begin the real selling process. All too often, however, this is where the HR practitioner lets himself or herself down. The quality of the sales pitch must be at least as high, in terms of graphics, delivery and general presentation, as the line manager might expect from an outside consultant. After all, that is what they will be making the comparison against.

Once the sale is made and the HR initiative implemented, there is a need for after-sales service. What precisely went well or badly? What lessons can be learned? What improvements can be made? What other initiatives can HR suggest that would reinforce the same business goals?

While all this is going on, the HR department can also make sure it advertises its wares effectively. Standard approaches include producing catalogues of training courses, or brochures of HR services, but more adventurous HR departments establish newsletters or magazines that not only detail what is on offer, but sell the benefits and explain why *they* are the right people to deliver them. Posters, audio tapes, videos, the employee newspaper, the annual report and articles in the local and national press are all additional useful vehicles for achieving a higher profile.

At the same time, it is important to build the department's reputation as a centre of excellence. That will come in part as a result of the quality of delivery. But there are other, visible signs that you can use to speed up the process. In one company, for example, managers receive a regular digest of the most recent thinking on management issues, culled from newly published books and magazines and from conferences around the world. By association, the HR department is recognised as a source of advanced ideas. A few HR departments, such as that at ICL (see Chapter 5), have demonstrated to the rest of the company that they, too, can achieve BS 5750 accreditation. Others are looking to use themselves as guinea-pigs for new management initiatives.

The language and concepts of marketing have a great deal to offer the HR function. They hold valuable lessons in how to position what the function offers in more or less hostile markets; how to focus efforts on those services which will have greatest impact on bottom line or business objectives; and how to capitalise on success. At the same time, effective marketing strategies will help HR gain the credibility it needs to have a greater say in the running of the business. What more could anyone ask?

Why market HR now?

To some extent, marketing is a simple question of survival. As more and more of the routine functions of personnel are passed out of house or on to line managers, the personnel function faces direct competition from outside suppliers, not all of them obvious competitors. Marketing techniques offer the best protection.

At Whitbread, for example, changes in legislation which

11

opened up the pensions market led to some employees opting out of company pensions in favour of personal pensions from the financial services sector. Whitbread's staff included a large number of young pub managers and part-time bar staff from the company's retailing divisions. It was largely in an effort to appeal to these typically young and mobile individuals that in 1991 Whitbread's pensions department decided to revamp its brochure.

What concerned Alan Bennet, the Whitbread group pensions manager, was that new employees frequently chose external pension schemes over the company's own schemes despite their favourable terms. He felt that in many cases new employees were making financially irrational decisions because they were unaware of the company's own portable pensions options.

The solution, the pensions department decided, lay in marketing the company scheme via a new-look brochure that would spell out the benefits, and focus attention on the need to plan for retirement – an issue often neglected by young people in the past. The brochure design and message was questioned, however, by HR professionals from Whitbread's retailing divisions. Says Dick Pearson, personnel director for Whitbread Inns: 'We felt it was rather dreamy, middle-aged stuff. We needed instead something more vibrant to appeal to the dynamic, aggressive younger people who manage our retail pubs and restaurants.'

Pearson and his HR colleagues suggested carrying out some internal market research on the brochure design among their line managers. 'The point that I made,' says Pearson, 'was that if the retailing HR departments were not completely convinced that the brochure was going to hit the target, it would affect how hard we pushed it, and with 90 per cent of Whitbread's total employees on the retail side, that could make a difference to the success of the initiative.'

It was agreed that Whitbread's own internal market research group should select a small sample of 16–18 retail line managers for an in-depth market research survey. The sample was chosen to reflect the range of Whitbread's retail outlets from traditional pubs to restaurants, hotels and off-licences and included single male and female participants as well as couples who manage a site together. An external interviewer was commissioned who had a good understanding of the Whitbread culture and the pubs and restaurant lifestyle. Interviews were conducted with line staff in July 1991. The results were a surprise.

The survey revealed that, although the HR experts were right to question the message of the brochure, which aimed to make employees think about pensions – something the survey showed they had already done – and although the design attracted some criticism, there was a bigger issue involved. Dick Pearson explains: 'We found that the brochure was just a side issue. What our people really wanted was someone to sit down with them and talk them through the pensions maze, and most importantly someone who would answer their questions. That's what they were getting from external pensions salesmen and that's what they wanted from us.'

The revelation has led to a radical rethink of pensions communication at Whitbread. Although a dedicated pensions sales staff is seen as unrealistic for the 3,000 outlets of the retail operation, pensions manager Alan Bennet is confident that, as a result of the market research, his department is better able to serve its internal customers. 'We looked at ways to put our employees in touch with the information they want,' he says. As a result the following steps were taken:

- The redesigned brochure is now issued to all new full-time employees.
- A pensions helpline is now in operation.
- The company operates a personal recommendation service with inputs by telephone or completed pro-forma.
- Pension contacts (local HR management and staff) are able to assist employees with their simpler questions, and redirect more complex matters to the pensions department.

Dick Pearson, who admits he was as surprised as everybody else by what the survey uncovered, believes the lesson for HR professionals is a simple one: 'Ask your internal customers what they want,' he says, 'otherwise, even with the best will in the world, you can miss the target by a mile and that's something none of us in HR can afford to do.'

Such is the power of market research. But quite simple marketing techniques can also be used to protect the market position of internal HR suppliers. For example, branding everything HR does from induction packs to procedural manuals, can help demonstrate to other functions that HR is adding value. It is far more difficult for line managers to ask what it is that HR contributes to the business when they regularly use high-calibre materials that they can see come from the HR function.

For example, the training department at the Woolwich Building Society brands all materials it generates for internal consumption with its own logo. This ensures that its brand is instantly recognisable within the company.

There are positive reasons, too, why the time is right for HR practitioners to market the function. For one thing, they are getting better at their own PR; at showing that they are qualified professionals, not paper pushers; at demonstrating that these qualifications are worth something, are of practical use and are relevant to line managers.

Recent surveys carried out by the IPM Chiltern Branch, for example, found that its members placed the HR function's contribution to the bottom line and the question, 'Are you the business partner your line managers expect?' at the top of a range of issues for discussion. The next priority, the surveys found, was 'the HR specialist as an internal consultant'.

To a certain extent, then, this suggests an awareness on the part of HR practitioners of a particular set of opportunities and threats facing HR in the mid-1990s that make the time right to raise its profile.

On the negative side, in-house HR functions need to defend themselves from a number of potential threats, including:

- the de-layering of management hierarchies and general down-sizing, which makes personnel practitioners vulnerable in the long-run;

- compulsory competitive tendering and market testing in the public sector;
- the devolution of traditional personnel roles to line management;
- the stigma attached to the function responsible for implementing redundancy programmes;
- the general trend towards outsourcing non-core functions.

On the positive side, opportunities include:

- the general move to people-based business strategies such as total quality management, and culture-change programmes to become more customer focused;
- the need for greater HR input into strategic planning to cope with specific issues such as skills shortages and an ageing population;
- the importance now placed on management development and training at all levels;
- the high profile afforded by initiatives such as Investors In People.

Increasingly, too, quality management techniques are now being applied to the people side of the business to raise the levels of service companies provide to their customers. Customer care has become the watch word of the 1990s. In many organisations, too, the personnel function is heavily involved in implementing the quality and customer care programmes aimed at beating the competition. HR practitioners who play an active role in these changes have a chance to integrate their departments more closely with the other 'core' functions. If they succeed, they will also be well positioned to drive the sort of value-added HR strategies which many business commentators claim will form the basis of competitive advantage in the future.

When The Royal Bank of Scotland introduced a customer care programme back in 1988, for example, it did so with the aim of gaining competitive advantage over its high-street rivals. In early 1987, the training department was asked to draw up plans to enhance customer service. But senior management rejected its initial proposals because they were not ambitious enough. Later that year, in conjunction with an external consultancy, training managers carried out a customer service audit which concluded that a major obstacle to any customer care programme lay in the bank's organisational climate. Employees needed an open, consultative, informative style of leadership where their enthusiasm and ideas would be welcomed, rather than the more autocratic style then in place.

The training department devised a two-year company-wide programme called 'Where People Matter', which involved a series of one-day courses for all employees and three-day courses for all managerial staff, including senior managers. In all, the courses lasted fifteen months and involved over 20,000 staff on 950 course programmes at a total cost of £2.5 million.

This programme, and managerial initiatives called 'Surprising the Customer' and 'Doing it Right', helped create a new organisational climate which is best described by the Japanese term *kaizen*, meaning an attitude of mind geared towards improvement. Through its early involvement in the service strategy the training department influenced the direction the strategy took. For example, the old quality circles were adapted to become 'service circles'. The profile of the training department was raised as a consequence.

HR departments are also more aware now than before of the need to measure both what they do and how they do it. In this way, they can show real improvements in the way they operate and the impact they have on the bottom line of the business. Increasingly, too, they realise that measurement is a vital tool in adapting HR processes to suit the real needs of internal customers.

For example, the personnel department at Joshua Tetley & Son developed an innovative recruitment strategy to support the company's customer service objectives. Personnel believed it was important to find people with a talent for service. It pioneered an approach based on the idea that some people have such a talent. These people have 'life themes' that are more appropriate to service than others, which means that because they draw greater personal

16

satisfaction from providing good service they are 'naturals' for jobs such as working in bars and restaurants.

According to one personnel manager at the company, 'People who have a high customer orientation want to keep winning a customer again and again. Providing excellent service is part of their mission in life; they feel the need to be good at it.' In its recruitment advertising, therefore, Tetley emphasises the qualities most important to customer-oriented managers. For example, they ask: 'Could you create an atmosphere where people can have a good night every night?' There has been a radical improvement in the quality of applicants as a result.

But it did not end there. To test the pay-offs of this rigorous approach to selection on service criteria, personnel carried out a detailed study of the business performance of managers recruited using the new selection research, compared to a control group of managers selected in the normal manner. Managers recruited conventionally had increased sales by 2 per cent per year over a five-year period. Those selected on service criteria achieved an average of 12 per cent. Conventionally recruited managers increased net profits by 8 per cent per year, those selected on service criteria by 17 per cent.

Personnel also compared the net profit of its 25 most talented managers (up 198 per cent over five years) with that of its bottom 25 (up 55 per cent). Among its conclusions from this exercise was that there would be a better pay-off from concentrating its efforts on helping the top performers perform even better, than from trying to drag the bottom performers up to the average. Naturally, these findings were communicated to senior management and other functions.

If you are still not convinced that the time is right to market HR, consider the following. The 1991 ITEM Group survey[1] found that fewer than 5 per cent of line managers interviewed thought that there were no benefits to be gained from a more proactive HR approach to internal marketing. A significant proportion also felt that HR should use marketing techniques to define its own role within the organisation – which will be music to the ears of many HR practitioners. The majority of HR professionals interviewed also spoke of the benefits of marketing their function in terms of clarifying the HR role and establishing ground rules for HR–line management interaction and areas of responsibility.

The combination of all these factors means that the case for actively marketing the HR function to other parts of the business has never been stronger. In particular we believe that HR functions can benefit greatly from the application of techniques embodied in customer care programmes, communications strategies, market research surveys and market analysis. These will all be covered in later chapters, but first let us turn to the 'idea' of marketing, and look at the marketing challenge facing HR in the second half of the 1990s and some general marketing techniques and principles.

The marketing challenge

According to the widely respected business writer Theodore Levitt:[2] 'Marketing is concerned with the idea of satisfying the needs of the customer by means of the product and the whole cluster of things associated with creating, delivering and finally consuming it.' He also noted that: 'It alerts us to a world of constant change where survival requires studying and responding to what people want and value, and quickly adjusting to choices provided by competition, which often comes from outside the industry in which it finally occurs'.

Levitt was referring to external markets, but, as the competition for resources within organisations continues to intensify, there are clear implications for the internal marketing of business functions today, and none more so than HR, where current opportunities and threats are finely balanced. Most significantly, however, the pendulum of competitive advantage is moving back towards strategies based on people. It is for internal HR departments to ensure that they, rather than external HR competitors or other internal functions, reap the rewards.

There are interesting parallels here with the information technology (IT) explosion of the 1980s which revolutionised almost every aspect of British industry, causing a large-scale internal redistribution of resources. During this period companies pursued competitive advantage through new technology, often at the expense of traditional skills. But the tightness of markets and the impact of changing demographics in the 1990s suggest that the wheel has now come full circle. In the very near future competitive advantage will increasingly belong to those organisations which achieve the optimal use of their human resources. For example, the rush to establish effective customer service programmes – supported by information technology, but seeking competitive advantage through people – is well under way.

The increasing emphasis on people strategies makes the business environment of the 1990s especially fertile for HR practitioners. But, just as the IT revolution was characterised by two distinct phases – a period of technology for the sake of technology, and a second phase that conferred real competitive advantage by delivering what its end users wanted – so, too, must HR practitioners in the turbulent 1990s be seen to deliver tangible results that add value to the business. Indeed, there is evidence now of a third phase in the IT revolution, with many companies questioning how much competitive advantage IT really confers. Some have concluded that the cost in many cases outweighs the benefits. It is a sobering thought for internal HR practitioners, too, that with the increasing emphasis on facilities management, whole IT functions, such as that at the Inland Revenue, are being subcontracted to outside suppliers. Elsewhere, much of the demand for IT solutions is now supplied by external consultancies which have succeeded in usurping the internal IT department's role.

All of which brings us back to the marketing challenge facing HR specialists today. Quite simply, it is the same as that which faces managers in all disciplines, that of self-promotion through high levels of professional competence to deliver *the right services, in the right place, at the right time and at the right price*. Or, to quote from a presentation given by Peter McCue, European personnel director Land Mobile Products Sector of Motorola: 'Right people, right place, right time, right cost.'

More specifically, HR practitioners have to find ways to get closer to their internal customers and to strengthen the customer–supplier relationship. To do so they will have to answer some fundamental questions about the role of HR in their organisations in the future.

Three different roles

In Sweden, a study by the Uppsala Institute of Human Resources Management (IPF)[3] identified three different roles for HR in the near future:

- a strategic role
- an internal consultancy role
- an internal services role.

A survey among 60 leading HR directors in Swedish service industries and the public sector conducted by the IPF in 1990 revealed how they spent their time that year and their expectations for 1992. Table 1.1, which appeared in an article by Magnus Söderström in *Personnel Management*, shows the results.

The table shows a clear trend away from the traditional service support role towards the strategy and consultancy roles. In part, the change from an administrative role to a more strategic focus for HR activities reflects structural changes in the Swedish economy as it moves away from a manufacturing base to one centred on service industries. At

Table 1.1
How personnel directors saw their role

	1990	1992
Strategic role	20%	32.5%
Consultancy role	32%	37%
Service/support role	47.9%	30.4%

Source: Hedlund, E. *et al.* 'HRM in the third wave', IPF, 1990.

the same time, the country is experiencing the effects of the world recession and a domestic decline in competitiveness. Because of these factors, Söderström notes, 'executive boards, managing directors and personnel managers have to try a number of different strategies to handle this situation'. The parallels with what is happening in Britain are clear.

In Sweden, these developments have fuelled debate among HR professionals about the path the function should follow. According to Söderström: 'One would be the professional, strategic path; the alternative would be non-professional and non-strategic.'

In the UK, too, the role played by HR functions in different organisations seems likely to change. That of an individual HR function will depend in part on its ability to meet the current needs of the organisation, but also on the path it chooses to follow.

The HR function's ability to 'sell' itself to the organisation either in a strategic role or as a support function will be greatly improved by a marketing plan. The design of such a plan requires a good grasp of some general marketing principles including:

- marketing mix
- internal SWOT analysis
- defining resources.

The internal marketing mix

The concept of the marketing mix is one much loved by marketers. Simply stated, it says that there are a number of components, or ingredients, which make up a successful marketing plan; the secret of success is to find the correct blend or 'mix' of those components.

Writing in *Marketing Business* (February 1990),[4] Nigel Piercy and Neil Morgan of the Cardiff Business School advocate the marketing mix concept as a starting point for looking at internal marketing strategies. Their analysis provides a useful general framework for marketing HR.

They take as the ingredients for the internal marketing

mix: product, price, promotion and distribution, which they define as follows:

- *product* – initially the strategies and plans that have been developed, but then also the values, attitudes and behaviour needed to make them work.
- *price* – the resources required, but also the opportunity cost of sacrificing competing projects and the psychological cost of adopting key values and changing the way jobs are done.
- *promotion* – communications, messages and media to inform, persuade and work on the attitudes of key personnel in the internal marketplace.
- *distribution* – not only the physical venues at which the product and promotion are delivered, but ultimately also the way human resources are managed by lining up training and recruitment behind strategy.

Achieving the right internal marketing mix, they say, depends on an analysis of strengths, weaknesses, opportunities and threats (SWOT) within the internal marketplace. We prefer to call this by its more conventional name of market analysis. For HR practitioners it will generally involve analysing the internal environment in which they operate, and setting this against the external picture of what is happening within the company's sector. At the same time, the notion of internal environment allows the HR practitioner to take account of another important factor: the culture of the organisation.

SWOT analysis of the internal environment

The 1991 ITEM survey showed that the organisational environment and culture in which personnel practitioners operate greatly affects their ability to market the function and to enhance the HR contribution to business objectives. In particular, it identified the following factors as critical to the success of efforts to market the HR function to line managers:

- *The image of HR within the organisation* – the perceived role and standing of the HR function will affect its ability to market new or existing services. Building a strong HR brand will be an important marketing strategy for many HR functions and one which will rely heavily on cultural perceptions.
- *The personal characteristics and communication skills of the HR director or equivalent* – HR credibility and standing with line managers is closely related to their perception of the HR professionals in charge. In many organisations HR practitioners underestimate the importance of the 'human' element of 'human resources'. Line managers are more likely to 'buy-in' to HR marketing where they see clear demonstration of human management skills at a senior level in the function.
- *The communications approach of the HR function* – the integrity and methods of communication employed between line managers and the HR function underpins the customer–supplier relationship and is critical to meeting customer needs.
- *The demonstrated performance of the HR function in critical areas recognised by line managers as important* – evidence suggests that the HR function's reputation and perceived competence with line managers is largely determined by its performance in a few key areas. Effective marketing will try to understand, satisfy and build on these primary customer needs.
- *The ability of the HR function to overcome both functional and geographical separation* – line managers in outlying sites frequently perceive themselves to be isolated from the centre. The credibility of any HR marketing proposition will be affected by the ability of the HR function to deliver its customer promise consistently. At the same time, this may be greatly hindered if HR continues to be seen by others as a head office function, or as one staffed by cultural 'interlopers' and 'outsiders'.
- *The ability of the HR function to add value to line managers by keeping them informed* – the efficient provision of up-to-date information about staff and the employment market is increasingly seen by line managers as a

primary role of the HR function. In addition, it is seen as an important strategic input that in the future could allow HR to redefine its own role and reposition itself in the internal marketplace.

To this, of course, must be added an analysis of sources of competition. Competitors include anyone who could either take over your responsibilities or tasks as a function, or make alternative claims on budgets currently or potentially assigned to you. They can be internal (for example the marketing or IT departments) as well as external.

Having identified sources of competition, you need to:

- assess their strengths, weaknesses and strategies
- decide when to use them as allies and when to compete for funds/responsibility
- monitor changes in their market position.

For the in-house HR function with its own marketplace to protect it will often pay to be collaborative with competitors rather than adversarial.

Defining the current resources

The next stage in the design of a marketing plan for the HR function is to determine how best to allocate available resources (the product and price components of the market-ing mix). To do so, you must have a clear understanding of the resources you currently command. All functions have limited resources, of course, but managerial and pro-fessional competence is judged by the way you use the resources you are allocated. There is no point, for example, in drawing up an elaborate marketing plan that cannot be implemented. All that such a move is likely to achieve is to confirm to other functions that HR is living in cloud cuckoo land. What must be achieved instead is a marketing plan that works. It is, after all, an end in itself. It sends an important message to the rest of the organisation about the way HR is marshalling its resources for the future.

An analysis of the resources available should include:

- a realistic view of current and future HR staff levels
- current programmes and budgets
- a realistic view of current in-house expertise, both in terms of areas and levels of expertise available
- the status of support materials, including training materials, procedures manuals etc. (Are they out of date? How soon will they need to be replaced? Do they meet the current and future needs of clients and customers? How do they compare with externally available materials in content and presentation?)
- information technology capability
- access to non-HR opinion formers within the organisation, who might be persuaded to act as 'ambassadors' for HR
- the availability and cost of using external suppliers to augment in-house resources
- the current stock of goodwill towards HR within the organisation
- the morale among HR staff and in the organisation at large.

Clearly, it will not be possible to attach a tangible value to all of these factors, but by reviewing them you should be able at least to get a feel for the sorts of resources that might be devoted to marketing.

The next step is to try to match the available resources with the marketing priorities to arrive at some clear marketing objectives. To do so effectively, however, you will need to carry out market research among your clients and customers. By consulting with customers, you can improve your success rate dramatically. If, for example, the resources exist to offer a new training programme to support line managers in achieving their performance targets, the main marketing effort could be directed there. Moreover, by focusing your efforts on involving line managers in the programme's design, you will improve the chances of it being successful. In this way, the high cost of introducing a new programme can more easily be justified to senior management.

The aims of HR marketing plans can be as varied as the marketing techniques and activities they encompass. In one organisation, for example, it might be as simple as trying to put a human face on HR, while in another it might be intended to radically redefine the HR role in the organisation. In still other organisations, where the HR function is currently in a state of flux, part of the marketing task may be to provide the function itself with a sense of identity.

At the same time, widespread decentralisation means that many traditional personnel responsibilities are now being passed to line managers. The ability of HR specialists in decentralised organisations to market their services as internal consultants will play an important role in determining their future contribution.

The HR functions in other organisations may want to use a marketing strategy to defend their position against a particular threat. With the onset of compulsory competitive tendering, for example, many public sector HR departments are only too aware of the need to communicate the value of the in-house HR function. The alternative, they know, is to remain vulnerable to external competition. Faced with the choice, many have opted to take the bull by the horns, rather than wait for it to trample them underfoot. By acting early they can secure their market for the future.

At Peterborough Priority Services (an NHS trust which is now part of North West Anglia Priority Services), for example, personnel has consistently led the way with new initiatives in the area of quality management. Before the organisation implemented its own (pre-government) patients' charter, for instance, the personnel director of the old health authority had successfully introduced an employee charter and a positive action programme based on the belief that 'carers should be cared for, too'. As a result of this and many other forward-thinking initiatives, the personnel department has successfully positioned itself within the culture of the organisations as 'an agent for change'. As such, its role is now both strategic and high profile.

In the coming chapters we will look at what other HR functions have achieved through careful market positioning, and at a range of techniques to help HR practitioners build partnerships with their internal customers. In Chapter 2, we will look specifically at what HR functions currently do to find out what their customers want; and at more effective ways to obtain customer feedback.

Checklist

We end this chapter with some questions; your answers will help you decide whether marketing techniques have anything to offer.

- What opportunities do you see for HR in your organisation now and in the future?
- What threats does HR face internally and externally?
- What are you currently doing to position HR to meet these opportunities and threats?
- Could marketing help?

2

What Do Our Customers Want?

This chapter was very nearly called 'Do we know what our customers really want?', but that might have encouraged some HR practitioners, who think that they do, to skip over it. That would have defeated the object because the next few pages are intended to make a point. That is, quite simply, that the more certain service providers are that they do not need to ask what customers think, both about the sorts of services they provide and about themselves as providers, the further from the mark they usually are.

A golden rule of marketing is to listen to customers. Here we have tried to present some useful and, we hope, stimulating ideas and techniques to help HR practitioners bridge the divide between themselves and their customers. Much of what follows is based on what HR departments have been able to achieve using research and marketing tools to support internal customer care programmes. In particular, it looks at the value of effective techniques for obtaining customer feedback as a means to find out what customers:

- really want
- really value
- really think of HR's contribution
- really think could be done to improve that contribution.

But let us look first at the picture that emerges from recent research into the HR–customer relationship.

A survey carried out by MORI in May 1992[1] among 110 senior HR professionals, drawn from the 500 largest companies in *The Times* 'Top 1000' and financial and public sector organisations, found that over a third (36 per cent) of HR departments do not have any formal system of identifying the requirements of their internal customers. Even fewer actually measure their performance, with 55 per cent having no measurement systems at all.

It further revealed that HR functions from public sector organisations are more likely to measure performance (60 per cent compared to the lowest score of 37 per cent, which was in manufacturing). The pressure in the public sector from competitive compulsory tendering is one reason why this might be so, but it is interesting, none the less, to see public sector organisations apparently leading the way.

Among those HR functions which do have systems to measure performance, the most common, according to the MORI findings, are formal reviews, undertaken internally, and personal meetings. The public sector is also more likely than the private sector to monitor customer satisfaction via the level of customer complaints, statistics and questionnaires.

The same survey also found that although such evaluation is not common practice in most organisations, 84 per cent of HR professionals are nevertheless convinced that their function contributes to the company's business success. And half of these went further, claiming they contributed 'to a great extent' despite the relative lack of hard evidence to support their views.

In a separate survey in April 1992,[2] MORI interviewed 527 full or part-time employees in a nationally representative sample. The findings from this survey indicate that, although HR's contribution to the success of the business is not viewed as positively by its customers as it is by its practitioners, more than half of all the employees interviewed saw HR as making a valid contribution. However, there is a distinct lack of personal knowledge. Only 38 per cent of employees, had 'a great deal or fair amount' of contact with their personnel or HR function. Even allowing for the fact that line managers have taken on many of the traditional personnel responsibilities, this is still a worryingly low level of personal contact if HR practitioners hope to know what their customers want.

Significantly, too, a little over half of the line managers interviewed said they did not have much contact with their HR department.

In an article in *Human Resources* Magazine[3] summarising the findings of these two surveys, Susan Walker, managing director of MORI Human Resource Research, makes the following observations:

'Despite seeing themselves as internal consultants/ suppliers, human resources professionals could do more to identify the needs of their "customers". . . There is a distinct "market" for the human resource professional among the 61 per cent of "customers" who have little or no dealings with them at present.'

'The good news', she adds, 'is that closer contact with those customers has benefits in helping them to see their human resource/personnel department in a more positive light.'

The 1991 ITEM survey[4] was targeted more closely at line managers and HR practitioners. Its findings suggest there is a general consensus among HR practitioners that line managers' feelings towards HR are a significant factor in determining the effectiveness of the HR role. At the same time, most of the HR practitioners interviewed agreed that the negative attitude of line managers often limits the ability of the HR function to market itself. The feeling behind their comments seems to be: 'Line managers do not realise how good we really are, or how valuable our contribution really is.'

While this may to a certain extent be true, it raises the question of whose fault that is. On balance, we would suggest, it is probably down to HR to blow its own trumpet.

Customer perception is all there is

Marketing theory is firmly rooted in the notion that service and performance are only as good as customers believe them to be. Marketing techniques open the door to influencing the way that line managers feel about HR, but what HR practitioners must grasp is that line managers inevitably see things from their own perspective. To improve their understanding of what line managers really want, HR practitioners must try harder to put themselves in the line managers' shoes. They should remember too, that no amount of complaining that HR is misunderstood or undervalued will alter the way they are seen by their customers. This is business, and the customer is right, if not all the time, then at least a good proportion of it.

Management writer Tom Peters[5] expressed it well when he said: 'Customers perceive service in their own unique, idiosyncratic, emotional, erratic, irrational, end-of-the-day and totally human terms. Perception is all there is.'

What Peters did not feel it necessary to say, but might well have added, is that the perceptions of the customer and those of the supplier can be very different. The reality, in as much as there is a reality in his view, probably lies somewhere between the perceptions of the two. But it is the perceptions of the customer that should dominate if the supplier wants to keep him or her satisfied. It is the gap between the perceptions of HR customers and practitioners that marketing should seek to address. We call it the service perception gap.

The customer service perception gap

There is nearly always a gap between how service providers think customers perceive their service and how they actually do perceive it. It is only by creating an effective dialogue with customers and clients that HR can close the perception gap which has for so long kept it at a distance from other business functions. Remember, too, that when dealing with customers, 'perception is all there is'.

A revealing section of the ITEM survey illustrates the point. HR practitioners were invited to evaluate their own performance in a number of areas. They were asked to assign a score to the service they provided both on their own account and as they thought line managers would rate them. Answers were then compared with scores given by a selection of line managers for the same performance criteria. In general, not only did HR professionals in more proactive HR departments score higher with line managers for overall performance, but they were also typically much closer in their evaluation of line managers' perception of their performance. The implication here is that HR functions which are more critical of themselves than their customers will be more likely to impress.

In organisations where the HR function was highly regarded among line managers, HR professionals frequently expressed dissatisfaction with their own performance levels in areas where line managers were satisfied, or identified weaknesses in HR where none was perceived outside the function. These findings suggest that HR functions which perform well are driven by a strong internal desire for continuous improvement that often outpaces the expectation of their customers. This, we believe, is an indicator of high service standards reflecting a strategically well placed HR function.

In organisations where the HR function had low credibility and poor standing among line managers, performance evaluation by HR practitioners was often considerably out of step with the views of line managers. HR practitioners in these organisations often insisted that the culture there made it difficult to be innovative. Whilst this may be true in the short term, our findings in other organisations suggest that cultural obstacles can be overcome in the long term, and the image of HR enhanced, by addressing the perception gap.

Taken overall, these findings, whilst not surprising, do serve to underline the importance of good communications between line managers and HR practitioners and the value of building closer relationships with customers. They also point to potential benefits from the application of market research techniques to identifying performance shortfalls and addressing line managers' priorities. One tool that has proved effective here is the customer dissatisfaction index[6] developed by The ITEM Group. This enables researchers to quantify the degree of dissatisfaction that customers feel, both in general and as regards specific incidents.

The comments of some of the line managers in our survey are also revealing for what they tell us about the criteria they use to evaluate HR performance. They included:

– Speed of response is my criterion for judging HR. When I need to know something I need to know it quickly, especially when it relates to personal problems of my staff.

– The most important impact of HR on my job is the way in which they meet my recruitment objectives. They take care of all first interviews and only bring me in at the second interview stage when they've whittled the candidates down to one or two good applicants.

– I don't need mollycoddling, but I need speed when it counts. There are times when HR can make or break my operation and that's when I need them to be there.

– HR should tell us what they can do for us and set service standards in the important areas as we do for our customers.

– What's important to me is that HR communicate the reasons for necessary changes to my staff. I judge HR by that criterion.

– I evaluate personnel performance on a few individual issues. The key issues are remuneration/incentives packages to attract and retain good people, competitive conditions of service to give us a competitive edge, smooth transfer of staff to lubricate the organisation and a good supply of high-calibre staff.

– Personally, I'm looking for HR to put a human face on the business plan.

– I judge HR by the same standards by which line managers are judged, whether they achieve objectives in the agreed time-scales.

That these comments cover such a wide range of issues indicates how difficult it is to second-guess customers. When you consider, too, that these comments are all from line managers (although admittedly from a variety of organisations), who are just one of HR's target audiences, it suggests that HR practitioners who want to know more about how they are viewed must get out and start talking to their customers. It is an important part of market research and it requires them to be more proactive in obtaining customer feedback.

Customer feedback

American management author Ron Zemke[7] said of customer feedback: 'There is no best way to listen to customers and no such thing as paying too much attention to customers' opinions and ideas. The only cardinal sin is to do nothing.'

For the purposes of marketing HR, market research techniques and techniques to obtain customer feedback are the same. There are five critical areas in establishing an effective system to obtain customer feedback:

- What do we need to know?
- Who should we ask?
- What methods should we use?
- Who should be involved?
- How should we use the information we collect?

Within these five areas are a number of key points which must be addressed in order to design a system that will provide the quality of information required. The MORI surveys indicate, however, that all too often customer feedback to HR practitioners is a random activity, if it happens at all. A more structured approach should consider the following points.[8]

What do we need to know?

- the clients' or customers' service needs
- how well we are meeting them – what we do well and what we do badly
- where we could add value by improving the service we provide.

Who should we ask?

- a cross-section of current customers
- a selection of potential new customers
- HR staff
- anyone who can throw light on the issues.

What methods should we use?

- informal listening and discussions
- focus groups

- written surveys
- telephone surveys
- formal customer visits
- open days
- encouragement of complaints
- customer 'hotlines'
- customer advisory panels.

Who should be involved?

- as many people as possible in the HR function
- as many HR customers and clients as possible.

How will we use the information?

- to make improvements
- to aggregate several factors into a larger one
- to offer new value-added services.

Once you know what customers think of the services HR provides and the ways in which they would like to see those services improved, it is vital to respond. In the coming chapters we will look at ways to improve HR products and services and to publicise those improvements to boost the standing of HR within the organisation. But first it is necessary to look at another marketing principle: market segmentation.

Market segmentation

Research about marketing HR (including our own) has tended to concentrate on the relationship between HR and line managers. Clearly, however, line managers are just one of several groups (albeit an important one) with whom HR practitioners must integrate their activities more closely. Moreover, as a group they are rarely homogeneous – differences in level, function, personality, even length of time with the organisation, will give them different sets of perceptions and different needs. The 'line manager' segment may in reality be a dozen or more sub-segments.

Market segmentation is about defining the different audiences that products and services are aimed at. It recognises that there are different customer groups defined by particular needs and wants. This is not an alien concept for HR practitioners. In its most basic form, it is something we all do subconsciously whenever we talk to anyone. We would not, for example, bore the managing director by explaining to him or her the finer points of a new procedure for line managers handling absenteeism, any more than we would try to explain to an employee on the shopfloor the shortcomings of the senior management succession plan. There would be no point. Similarly, marketing activities, including the design of HR programmes, should address clearly targeted audiences.

By identifying precisely what the preferences of a particular segment or cluster are, and whom it is likely to include, and by prioritising between different market segments, HR can greatly improve its effectiveness.

Conventional consumer marketing views market segments in terms of customer profiles. So, for example, it might define the characteristics of a particular segment by looking at factors such as age, sex, disposable income, marital status, number of children or geographical location. A good illustration is the way that car manufacturers now view the vehicle market. They see it as made up of several distinct market segments, such as prestige cars, medium-sized family cars, small cars and commercial vehicles (vans and trucks), and target and market their offerings accordingly. So, for example, if we look at advertising – which is one component of the marketing mix – a car manufacturer's television advertising is made up of a number of different commercials each aimed at a distinct market segment. Commercials are targeted to appear with programming that is likely to be watched by a large proportion of the market segment they are aimed at.

By applying the same sort of approach to its internal market, HR too will be able to define its market segments and design products, services and promotional materials that meet the needs of customers and clients within those segments more closely. For one thing, it is far easier to meet the narrow requirements of a distinct market segment than it is to design catch-all solutions for everyone.

Typically, broad HR market segments might include:

- the board of directors
- senior managers
- line managers
- employees
- individual functions (eg IT or research and development), where there is a distinctive set of problems or development needs.

Within these, there will be further sub-markets, such as:

- high flyers
- plateaued managers
- line managers with problems such as high staff turnover, skills shortages or overmanning
- women returners
- racial or sexual minorities.

The real power of market segmentation is that it enables HR practitioners to take a more strategic look at their internal marketplace. So, for example, new training programmes can be designed around the real needs of a given segment, in the knowledge that there is a demand for them. Similarly, where it is no longer cost effective to provide a certain level of service to a declining market segment, it can be reduced. At the same time, HR practitioners will be better able to promote their ideas within the organisation if they pitch them at the right audiences.

One personnel function that has successfully applied market segmentation to its internal clients and customers is Rothmans. In 1991, the personnel department at the UK-based tobacco company was involved with a major relocation programme. Helene Coxhead, a former manager at Rothmans International Tobacco and now a marketing and management consultant, was on secondment to personnel at that time. 'People forget about segmenting internal audiences,' she says. 'They tend to all get lumped together

. . . The relocation documentation the personnel department had produced was basically a policy document for personnel managers and senior management. The people who needed the information most, the employees being relocated, got the least out of it. What these people really needed was something they could take home and share with their families, not 50 pages of policy.'

Coxhead and the personnel team working on the relocation programme felt that the best help package would be one that gave employees enough information to empower them to make their own decisions, while allowing personnel staff to retain control and reduce the problems for themselves. They favoured something written in an upbeat style which would make relocating exciting and understandable. It should begin, they decided, by congratulating the relocating employee on his or her new appointment.

The team analysed the audience segments and their informational requirements from the relocation package. The key audiences were:

- the board (which had to agree the policy)
- senior personnel managers (the cost centre which held the budgets)
- administration (including external advisers such as solicitors)
- relocating employees (who needed something practical and upbeat to boost morale).

As a result of this analysis, the team produced three documents. The board and the senior managers were treated as one audience as they required the same information. The administrators received another document containing the level of information they needed. And the relocating employees received an upbeat document they could share with their families. To keep costs down, the documents were produced on a word processor, but they were bound with covers bearing the distinctive Rothmans crest to add credibility and a corporate identity.

In another case, the HR department at Three Valleys Water Services used market segmentation to introduce a system of appraisal and performance-related pay into the company for the first time. The department knew that it would have to do a hard sell to the various market segments affected if it wanted the new system to stick. The right marketing mix would involve components aimed at each of the different audiences. In particular, they wanted to provide: advance information for all employees; training for the people who would have to run the appraisals; a vehicle to market the changes to staff at all the company's sites; and a means to brief union representatives.

The solution they arrived at was to provide an explanatory booklet for all employees; a series of training courses for all those who would be carrying out appraisals (from senior management down to supervisor level); a series of road-shows to all sites; and a two-day course for union representatives. The roadshow component consisted of two events at each of the company's sites, targeted on the concerns of employees. The first addressed the question, 'What is expected of you at appraisals?' and the second, 'What is performance-related pay and how will it affect your pay cheque?'

One of the most innovative parts of the way HR handled the briefing process was its willingness to involve union representatives in an open manner. A two-day course was organised for them, using outside specialist consultants and with the head of personnel present.

In another case, civil engineering and water treatment specialists Biwater wanted to communicate the benefits of the company's pensions package to younger employees. Concerned that they would not read printed materials, a video presentation was seen as the best way to reach this market segment. An informative and entertaining video was therefore produced and distributed among this target group.

Clients vs customers

In discussing the applications of market segmentation to HR, there is an important distinction to be drawn between clients and customers. Customers are the recipients of HR services, whereas clients are the people within the organisation who 'buy' the service or influence the definition of requirements. So, for example, typical clients would be line managers who send their staff (the customers) on training courses run by HR.

The difference between clients and customers has important implications when looking at market segments, particularly when a new programme or service is concerned. HR needs to be clear that a demand for something among customers does not necessarily translate into a demand among the 'payers' – the clients. It is quite likely, for instance, that a great many employees would welcome the introduction of a training course in scuba diving. Line managers, however, might not view it in the same light.

On the other hand, scuba diving was one of the activities Rover Learning Business (RLB) helped fund when it introduced a scheme called Rover Employee Assisted Learning (REAL). The scheme offered £100 towards the cost of a new learning experience for every Rover employee. According to Rover's HR director, David Bower, the REAL programme was very important as a statement of intent to signal to employees that the creation of RLB marked a move away from the traditional idea of training towards the notion of learning. The client in this case was the senior management team which authorised the strategic switch from training to learning.

As well as a great many courses in languages and computing skills, take up of REAL included courses in sheep husbandry, navigation of internal waterways and scuba diving as well as many courses of golf lessons. 'REAL was a breakthrough because it was for everyone,' says David Bower. 'It switched the emphasis from training to learning. It was important, too, that whereas in the old days we'd have had a rule book to say what was allowed, the new way was to leave it to line managers to sign off applications.'

Checklist

We end this chapter like the last, with some questions. This time they are aimed at getting you to think about how customer-aware you are.

How well do you believe the HR function in your organisation, or you personally, perform on the following?

- Do you always consider the customer's point of view when taking operational decisions?
- How frequently do you modify procedures to meet customer requirements?
- Do you welcome complaints as an opportunity to make improvements?
- Do you actively measure customer satisfaction on a regular basis? Do you know the size of the service perception gap and have a plan to reduce it progressively?
- Do you personally make a point of listening to customers, preferably at the site where they work?
- Do you personally try to set an example of being customer-oriented?
- Do you discuss customer-satisfaction issues with HR staff?
- Do you make a point of acknowledging/rewarding customer-responsive behaviour?

PART II
Changing the Reality

3

Improving the Services We Provide

There are two levels at which marketing must work, if it is to bring about a change in the way the HR function is positioned within an organisation. It must influence first the reality of HR performance, and second customers' perceptions of HR performance.

At the first level, marketing techniques can be used to change the actual products and services HR provides to its customers. For example, techniques for obtaining customer feedback (market research) provide the function with information about the criteria by which customers evaluate HR's contribution. These criteria can then be used to prioritise its efforts.

At the second level are customers' perceptions about HR performance – in other words, how they think about HR. These are based on their understanding of what the function does. Over time, improvements in real performance will filter through the culture of the organisation to bring about a matching shift in customers' perceptions.

For example, if customer feedback indicates that a key performance indicator for a given market segment (say line managers in outlying sites) is the speed with which queries are handled, then an effective marketing response should:

- First, address the issue itself by reviewing and improving performance in this area in line with customer requirements. For example, if line managers want the reassurance of a telephone acknowledgement of their query within 24 hours, followed by the answer within three days, HR should put systems in place to ensure that performance meets these requirements.
- Next, consolidate the performance improvement using an appropriate measurement (perhaps the number of queries answered within this time-frame compared with the number of failures to do so)

- When the real performance improvement is solid (ie 100 per cent, or near), the second phase of marketing can begin to work on perceptions. Typically, this might involve informing customers of the improvement by publicising the new performance targets in this area, or publishing service guarantees (see below). The first thing line managers will do is test its validity, so it is essential to deliver what is promised as soon as the target is made public. Perception should then be reinforced by addressing other key performance indicators in the same way. If line managers perceive that performance has indeed been improved, overall HR credibility will be enhanced, paving the way for improving service in other key performance indicators.

Once the ball is rolling, the two will automatically reinforce each other – better performance improves the image of HR which in turn gives the function greater freedom to introduce new products and services or make further improvements to existing ones. But because perceptions tend to lag behind the reality, it is useful to start by addressing them separately.

In Chapters 5, 6 and 7 we will look at ways to influence customers' perceptions. But since it is a prerequisite to changing perceptions, we will look first at techniques to change the reality, including improving the products and services HR provides, professionalising the HR function and gaining a reputation for quality. In this chapter we are looking at ways to improve the products and services HR provides, using the following tools and techniques:

- targeting critical performance indicators
- the service improvement cycle
- customer service contracts
- managing customer complaints
- customer recovery strategies.

Targeting critical performance criteria

The most effective strategies to change the reality of HR performance will be those which successfully identify and target areas of HR performance that are a priority with clients. We suggest the model in Figure 3.1.

It is fundamental to the success of this model that HR practitioners work closely with clients to define critical performance indicators which matter from their perspective and not simply from the HR viewpoint.

Failure to achieve agreed targets without good reason may undermine HR credibility and adversely affect future HR initiatives. It is essential, therefore, to address performance shortfall in critical areas where HR commitment is strong and to consolidate performance gains before moving on to other initiatives. The 1991 ITEM survey indicates that, if the HR function is seen to be getting the basics right, it will have a much freer hand to implement more ambitious initiatives later. It is worth repeating here that when it comes to identifying critical performance indicators, customer perception is all there is. So, for instance, if line managers expect the HR function to set an example in terms of the speed with which telephones are answered, then that is a meaningful performance indicator, regardless of the importance HR practitioners attach to it for its own sake.

Similarly, at the other end of the spectrum, new ways to measure the impact of HR initiatives, especially training, are likely to be more meaningful for line managers if they are seen to measure 'real performance'. There is clear disillusionment about 'happy sheet' approaches as a means of assessing the effectiveness of training and a growing acceptance that 'real' measurements must relate to subsequent job performance. A crude measure of the effectiveness of sales staff training might therefore be based on the subsequent sales figures of the individual who received the training, instead of whether they felt the training was valuable.

Evidence shows that more rigorous measures of training effectiveness are long overdue in many organisations. (During the year 1986/7 British employers spent £18 billion on training according to figures published in 1989 in the report *Training in Britain*[1] by the Training, Enterprise and Education Directorate of the Employment Department, but

Figure 3.1 The process solutions

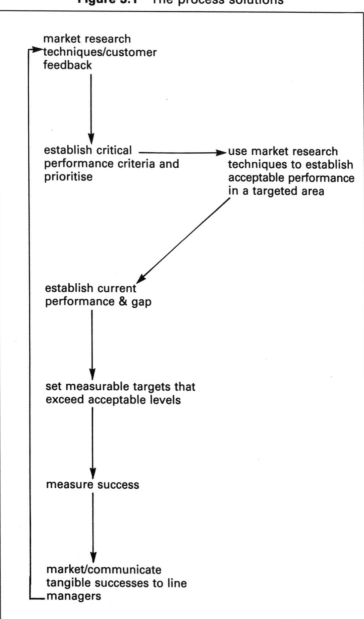

only 19 per cent of employers who undertook training during that period could list its benefits, and only 40 per cent took the time to cost out their investment.)

From another perspective, the lack of effective evaluation for training and across a range of other HR activities can be seen as responsible for keeping HR in a subordinate, non-strategic role within many organisations. Senior management is inevitably concerned with looking at costs in relation to benefits delivered by functions such as finance, marketing and operations. They have been largely unable to do so in relation to training and HR generally. The result has been a lack of hard management information which has contributed to a lack of belief in the ability of HR to input at a strategic level.

If we return to the training example, this can be broken down into assessment in three phases:[2]

- *immediate* – this relates to changes in knowledge, skill or behaviour immediately after a training experience. In particular it should seek to establish whether the training has been effective in communicating the message. Have people learned the skills you were setting out to teach? Do they understand what is required of them? Have they been equipped with the necessary behaviours to be able to implement the learning?
- *intermediate* – this refers to evidence that knowledge, skill and behaviour which has been learned is being put into use on the job. In other words, can the trainee, and his or her manager and colleagues, identify a change in behaviour, skill and attitude as a result of his or her attendance?
- *long term* – this refers to the long-term effectiveness of the individual, the work unit and the organisation as a whole. The ultimate evaluation is difficult and only possible if the training in the first instance has been related to the real corporate, strategic and business needs of the organisation. What HR is trying to evaluate is whether the individual subsequently makes a real contribution to the business needs of the organisation, or whether training has just been a comfortable and enjoyable experience which has brought about little change.

Evaluation is about determining the value of the training delivered. It should seek to assess:

- the effectiveness of the training
- the effectiveness of the learning process – in other words whether the trainees have learned what trainers set out to teach them
- whether that learning has been applied
- whether the applied learning has brought about the changes required in relation to attitudes, skill or behaviour.

By considering training within the context of the three phases outlined above, it should be possible to design and apply a range of evaluation techniques appropriate to each phase. These might include:

- post-course assessments
- pre- and post-course tests
- management briefing
- management debriefing
- questionnaires
- appraisals
- promotability
- assessment/development centres
- repertory grids
- surveys
- trainer interviews
- trainer-observed behaviour
- participant observation
- records of performance
- action plan follow-up.

These methods are shown with their possible applications in Table 3.1.

The Holy Grail of HR

At the macro level, a clear-cut correlation between measured HR performance and profitability has long eluded

Table 3.1

Selection of the most appropriate evaluation techniques

Evaluation techniques	Trainer requirements					
	Rapid immediate feedback	Considered but early feedback	Medium-term considered feedback	Long-term results	Assessment of skill changes	Assessment of attitude/ behaviour change
1. Post-course assessments	✓					
2. Pre- & post-course tests		✓				
3. Management briefing		✓	✓			
4. Management debriefing			✓			
5. Questionnaires				✓		
6. Appraisals					✓	✓
7. Promotability				✓	✓	✓
8. Assessment/development centres					✓	✓
9. Repertory grids				✓	✓	✓
10. Surveys			✓	✓		
11. Trainer interviews		✓				
12. Trainer-observed behaviour	✓				✓	✓
13. Participant observation	✓					
14. Records of performance				✓		
15. Action plan follow-up						

HR practitioners. Writing in the *Financial Times* on 17 August 1992,[3] David Goodhart went so far as to call the ability to demonstrate that they add value in a similar way as other functions 'the Holy Grail of personnel management'.

Researchers from Lancaster University and the University of Wales, however, claim to have found the Holy Grail by establishing an 'association' between HR policy and profit.

The researchers studied five HR activities – recruitment and selection, management education, performance appraisal, reward and remuneration, and company career planning – and looked at how they were practised across 60 UK manufacturing companies.

The measures used were: how systematically they were conducted; how well integrated they were with each other; how well integrated they were with corporate strategy; and how meritocratically they were applied. They found that financially successful companies scored above average on all four measures. A particularly strong relationship was found between financial performance and the integration of HR policies with corporate strategy. Despite these evangelical teachings, however, Goodhart points out that their findings may well owe more to tautology than the Eucharist since well-run companies are generally more successful than badly run ones and are more likely to have well-managed HR policies too. In effect then, until a macro study makes the HR contribution at the bottom line stick, it falls to individual HR functions to find their own Holy Grails by making the sorts of measurements described earlier for training work.

The service improvement cycle

The service improvement cycle in Figure 3.2 is a simple model designed to focus attention on the eight components of service improvement. Its chief merit lies in stimulating HR practitioners to think through the processes involved in constructing HR systems which support those who work within the HR function to become more market-oriented.

Figure 3.2 The service improvement cycle

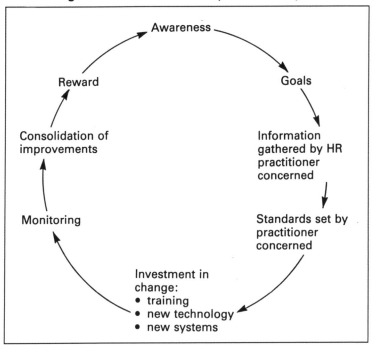

The main difference between the sorts of systems needed to support performance improvements for different market segments will typically be the seniority of the HR practitioner involved and the method by which they deliver the improvement. So, for example, we would expect senior HR professionals to be closely involved with a drive to improve the HR services provided to senior management. This would probably be delivered through close, one-to-one interactions with targeted senior managers. At lower levels in the organisation, however, local HR managers and staff should be the main movers. The critical element is to involve the service deliverer directly at the point of contact with the targeted customer or client. In this way, the HR practitioner who must ultimately deliver the improved service is empowered to do so. After all, it is pointless to have senior HR managers promising levels of service that cannot be achieved by the HR practitioners on the ground. Instead, senior HR managers should concentrate on:

- improving HR performance with senior management clients
- creating a service culture within the HR function as a whole
- empowering HR service deliverers by providing training, investment and strategic direction.

The effectiveness of the service improvement cycle model can be greatly increased if it is used in conjunction with the next technique – the customer–service contract.

Customer–service contracts

A number of HR functions in UK organisations have already implemented customer–service contracts with internal customers as the basis of developing closer customer–supplier relationships. Again, it is vital to involve service deliverers in the process of negotiating the service contract.

In a presentation paper to the Manchester Business School, Ron Zemke and Chip Bell[4] suggest that any customer–service contract involves promises made to customers which:

- make a noticeable difference to those customers
- have value in the customer's eyes
- are meaningful to the people who have to deliver them
- can be delivered.

They outline four factors which research in America has shown distinguishes the successful delivery of high-quality service:

- a focus on understanding of customers' wants, needs and expectations
- a well-conceived vision or plan for delivering service

- customer-oriented systems for delivering service
- customer-oriented staff.

The following is suggested by American management writers Berry and Parusuraman[5] as a checklist for designing customer-service contracts:

- *reliability* – the ability to provide what was promised dependably and accurately
- *assurance* – the knowledge and courtesy of employees and their ability to convey trust and confidence
- *empathy* – the degree of caring and individual attention provided to customers
- *responsiveness* – the willingness to help customers and provide prompt service
- *tangibles* – the physical facilities, written matter and appearance of staff.

A service strategy statement is an alternative approach to a detailed contract. It is a statement of general intent which creates a focus for all service activities. It can also provide a valuable starting point for creating a customer-service contract later. Among the questions it should address are:

- What counts most to our customers?
- What will count tomorrow?
- What can we do with our service that customers really notice?
- How do customers see us?
- What actions can we take to improve our services and to improve customers' perception of the HR function?

One organisation that practises what it preaches is management consultancy KPMG Peat Marwick, which introduced internal service contracts between HR and consultants in 1991. HR works closely in teams with KPMG's consultants to provide an added-value internal support function. HR initiated the contracts to ensure that it was providing what internal customers required, and to obtain a clearer picture of their priorities. The contract takes the form of a document that lists activities and performance measures such as turnaround times and responsibilities. Customer expectations are identified and set at face-to-face meetings between HR and consultant teams.

Service guarantees

We have all observed the power of a service guarantee promising 'satisfaction or your money back'. Such guarantees – if you have the systems in place to honour them – can be potent consumer marketing tools, but they can also be used to reinforce internal marketing campaigns.

An American company, Creative Professional Services (CPS), which provides direct-marketing services, created a service guarantee between its sales team and the production department. Sales people discuss ideas for direct-mail materials with prospective clients and write down the details, which they give to the account managers for production. Before the service guarantee was created, the company found it difficult to pinpoint how many mistakes resulted from poor information transfer between the two departments, but the service guarantee gave staff an incentive to identify and remedy common mistakes. The components of the CPS service guarantee provide a good starting point for similar ones between HR and its internal customers. They are:

- the *promise*, which can be specific, such as 'We will deliver x services by y date', or sweeping. The CPS sales people promised to give account managers all the information they needed to do their job.
- the *payout*, which usually takes the form of 'If I fail to deliver, I will give you x.' This is where the internal guarantee differs from the classic consumer guarantee. Money is not usually appropriate to the internal transaction, and the payout is not intended to punish offenders so much as to reward employees for picking up on errors. CPS used a choice of payments for production staff who identified incomplete specifications from sales, including

the sales person buying the production employee lunch or singing a song of his or her choice at the next sales meeting.
- The *invocation procedure*, which should make activating the internal guarantee easy. CPS employees deliver a simple invocation form to the author of the mistake.

Benefits from the internal guarantee included the creation of a standard 'job launch form' for sales staff to record crucial details, which helped to reduce small but potentially costly mistakes.

Managing customer complaints

There is, of course, another vital ingredient in building the sort of effective dialogue with clients and customers that is required to improve HR performance: how you react to negative feedback. This usually takes the form of complaints.

Far from being a nuisance, complaints – if they are properly managed – are probably the best source of information about what irritates clients and customers. And because they invite a response, complaints present an ideal opportunity to change a negative perception into a positive one. That is why a mechanism for collecting and reacting to complaints is an integral part of any customer service strategy. However, it is an area that is frequently neglected.

Theodore Levitt[6] wrote: 'One of the surest signs of a bad or declining relationship with a customer is the absence of complaints. Nobody is ever *that* satisfied, especially not over an extended period of time. The customer is either *not* being candid, or *not* being contacted.'

A report by researchers at Technical Assistance Research Programme Europe (TARP) found that there were significant benefits to responding well to complaints. TARP looked at how customer loyalty is influenced by a company's approach to complaints and its performance in recovering from mistakes. It claims that on average:

- 25 per cent of the customers of any service organisation are dissatisfied
- 4 per cent actually complain
- 60 per cent of those who complain will remain loyal if the organisation responds even if it does not do much
- 70 per cent will remain loyal if the problem is satisfactorily resolved
- 30–50 per cent of those who do not complain will switch to another supplier if one is available

TARP looked at five service scenarios and examined the customer's willingness to use the service provider again in each case. They found that customers who complain but are not happy with the outcome of their complaint feel worse about the service providers than those who do not bother to complain at all. Customers whose problems are recovered well are almost as likely to stay with the service provider as those who have never had a problem in the first place.

Good recovery pays off in terms of word-of-mouth advertising as well. The TARP findings suggest that a satisfied customer will tell five others, while an unhappy customer will tell ten. They also indicate that a customer who has experienced good recovery will tell three others about it.

Clearly, good service recovery works in retaining customers, while poor service recovery is not simply useless but can be very damaging. Not only does poor recovery reinforce customers' negative impressions of the service provider, it also aggravates them even more by wasting their time.

The key elements in an effective complaints system can be summarised as:

- Make it easy and comfortable for customers to tell you when they are unhappy.
- Provide rapid feedback and response.
- Use the information gathered to stimulate changes in systems, procedures, equipment, environment and behaviours.

Remember, too, the point that Levitt makes: just because

customers do not complain it does not mean that they are satisfied. This is particularly true of internal customers who might be expected to voice their dissatisfaction loudly because of the difficulty of going elsewhere, but in fact are more likely simply to accept the problem and try to work around it. This makes it all the more important to have systems in place which actively encourage complaints and are supported by customer recovery techniques.

But many internal functions make it difficult for customers to complain. They may ask for reactions, but in such a way as to protect themselves from hearing about any real problems. In one large manufacturing company, for example, line managers were so unimpressed with the internal HR function that rather than complain about poor recruitment delivery they brought in external recruiters, paid for out of their own budgets. This was only discovered by the HR function later when, as a major marketing exercise – which signalled its willingness to tackle its shortcomings – it conducted detailed surveys among its supposedly captive customers. HR has since radically redefined its role.

Typically, customers of HR departments with low credibility will have low expectations of the products and services it provides. As a result, they will not waste their own time by complaining. If complaints *are* made, the HR managers will tend to hide or repress them, for fear that, if they come to light, they will affect their performance ratings. Nor is this head-in-the-sand attitude confined to internal suppliers with captive audiences. Some organisations spend thousands of pounds on ineffectual, rhetorical public-relations exercises disguised as market research. The following cautionary tale illustrates the point.

A high street bank sent its personal banking customers a questionnaire about service standards. Perhaps it was a worthy exercise from the bank's point of view, yet the questions, with their smug assumptions that all was well, gave no opportunity for customers to bring up their real, and quite substantial, service problems. One of the bank's customers commented: 'The questionnaire asked about degrees of staff politeness, when my experience had been of degrees of staff rudeness. It asked if tasks were being done promptly, while I was fighting to have them done at all. Did the bank inform me promptly of new services? Sure they often sent advertising, but they never bothered to mention that they had moved my account, changed my sort code, invalidated my cheque book, cancelled my overdraft provision and doubled my charges – all things that interested me just a little more than new services.'

Successful HR functions, by contrast, actively encourage customers to complain, as they are confident that their staff and systems are capable of resolving the problem. So all complaint-inducing methods must be handled with care. If your perception of reality is too far removed from your customers', questionnaires such as that sent out by the bank in the example above can appear at best as thinly disguised promotional material.

How to encourage complaints

Manage the environment for complaining

- Tell internal customers and clients you want their comments, and why.
- Convince them you will do something about the complaints (and mean it).
- Make the atmosphere for complaining comfortable – one where internal customers do not have to put themselves out to tell you what is wrong.
- Provide the tools to make complaining easy. Provide a help desk, or at least put your telephone number on all your communications. Quite incredibly, some organisations still neglect to do this even when corresponding with external customers.

Manage the process for complaining

- Make the complaints process a priority activity with HR staff, and explain why.
- Encourage HR staff to be open about complaints. They

represent an opportunity rather than a threat, so support rather than punish.

- Build awareness among HR staff that complaints mean that customers are interested in what HR does.
- Be proactive – approach the customer; take the first or more difficult step yourself.

Manage the outcome of complaints

- Aim for immediate customer satisfaction.
- Empower HR staff to react to resolve complaints quickly.
- Measure and analyse complaints to see where you can improve products and processes in the medium term.
- Keep the customer informed about improvements for long-term customer satisfaction.

Be proactive   Some excellent service providers would never dream of waiting for a customer complaint if they spotted an error themselves. As a restaurant customer once told us: 'A waiter once whisked a meal out from under me with effusive apologies, before I had had a chance to lay eyes on the meal. The swirl of the potatoes and the angle of the parsley garnish was not up to his standards. Perhaps it was all show, but I could only admire his perfectionism.' By the same token, one HR director we spoke to said that he was unhappy with the current recruitment procedures used by the company, even though line managers interviewed said they were satisfied by HR performance in this area. The HR director concerned said that he intended to hold consultations with line managers to review the recruitment system and upgrade standards. In so doing, it is likely that he would achieve much the same effect as the waiter in the example above.

Manage service recovery   Once you have recognised the need for recovery, you must also look hard at how you are going to manage the recovery process, and in particular at how you will deal with service problems proactively.

As we have seen, managing the recovery process also calls for staff who have been empowered to react to customer

61

Figure 3.3 Customer recovery process

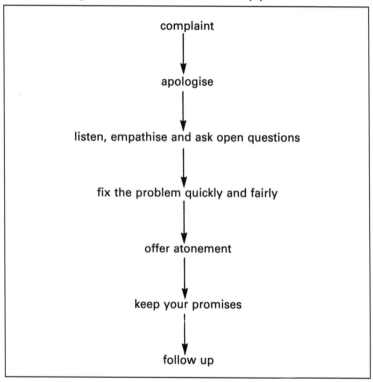

complaint

apologise

listen, empathise and ask open questions

fix the problem quickly and fairly

offer atonement

keep your promises

follow up

needs, and adequate measuring and monitoring systems. Approaches will vary from HR function to HR function, but some general principles are covered in the next section.

Customer recovery strategies

American management authors Zemke and Bell[7] define customer recovery as: 'returning an aggrieved customer to a state of satisfaction after a service or product breakdown has occurred'. They offer the model in Figure 3.3.

Service recovery plays an important role in enhancing the image of HR because service slips can so easily undermine what has already been achieved. Without systems for dealing with mistakes, a strategy to raise the HR profile can all too often become a question of one step forward and two steps back. Initiatives to market HR are especially vulnerable early on when image gains are still fragile. To avoid this problem, it is important to get the basics right. An HR department that is not good at delivering customer service will not be in a position to implement good recovery strategies. If you do not deliver well, you will not recover well.

Checklist

- Do you have a clear idea of the nature of the service you are trying to deliver?
- Do you know who your customers are and what they value from your service?
- Have you agreed key performance indicators with each major customer segment?
- Are your resources up to the challenge of meeting your performance targets?
- Can you recognise when things are most likely to go wrong?
- Do you have strategies in place to cope when they do?
- Are HR staff empowered to take the necessary action?
- Do you have systems to encourage complaints?
- Do you make use of complaints for customer recovery and for continuous improvement?

4

Professionalising the HR Department

HR has come a long way in the past ten years. But one question overshadows much of what has been achieved. Time and time again, frustrated by their lack of influence over strategic decisions, HR practitioners find themselves asking: 'Why does HR still have such a poor image in so many organisations?'

The answer, of course, is far from simple. But research suggests that the low standing of HR within many organisations is an important factor in restricting its input into strategic decisions. There is an unwillingness on the part of senior management and other functions to truly accept HR as a profession in its own right, or to accept HR practitioners as professional managers. One only has to look at the numbers of lawyers and accountants on the one hand and generalists on the other on the boards of British companies, compared with the number of HR professionals in similar positions of influence, to see the effect this has on strategic input.

'Personnel directors should not automatically expect a place on the board,' Powergen's chairman Sir Graham Day was reported as saying in *Personnel Management*.[1] Speaking at the annual conference of IPM Bristol, Day said that no one should be on a company's board in a solely representative capacity. They should not be appointed because of their managerial function but more for their breadth of experience. He cited as an example Cadburys Schweppes, of which he is also chairman. 'Currently the senior personnel executive is a main board member. His predecessor was not. This is no reflection on the personnel-related skills of either. Rather it reflects, in the case of the present incumbent, an educational and managerial breadth and experience which goes beyond the personnel function.'

The 1991 ITEM survey[2] included in-depth interviews with

over 120 line managers and HR professionals and found that, while few of those within the profession doubt the contribution HR could make at the strategy level, HR frequently lacks the clout to have a significant impact on the direction of the business. As a result, HR directors are either marginalised on strategy issues, or excluded from the boardroom altogether. Our research also indicates that HR functions that are able to overcome the image problem by demonstrating the value of their professional expertise have a far greater chance of repositioning themselves in the internal marketplace to realise their strategic potential.

But professionalism doesn't begin and end with senior HR practitioners; just like the lettering in seaside rock, it must run right through the HR function. At the same time, HR practitioners need to demonstrate that as well as being functional experts they can be professional managers.

The comment of one line manager in the ITEM survey illustrates the point: 'Personnel is seen as inefficient, not doing its job and spreading itself too thin. To win the confidence of line managers it would have to demonstrate it can run its own show in a businesslike way.' His view is not untypical.

In trying to pinpoint the reasons behind the HR image problem, the ITEM survey indicated three important factors:

- First and most significantly, line managers find it difficult to quantify the benefits HR brings to the business. As a consequence, it continues to be seen simply as a support function, rather than adding value where it counts – at the bottom line.
- Secondly, HR is still seen as a 'soft' discipline in many organisations. At its worst, it is regarded as the dumping ground for all non-core functions. Allied to this is the problem that HR is frequently seen by other functions as an interloper or outsider because it has not been expected to meet the same sorts of hard performance targets as they have. Personnel professionals have therefore tended to be seen as maintainers rather than strategic thinkers.
- Finally, in many organisations, there is a genuine 'sins of

the father' problem to overcome. This means that in spite of the 'people are our greatest asset' rhetoric from top management, a legacy of lacklustre HR performance in the past makes many organisations resistant to opportunities to achieve real competitive advantage through people.

As a result of these three factors, the survey report concluded: 'HR fails to develop value-added elements of its role to their full potential, remains largely misunderstood, or finds its approaches rejected by front-line management.'

Importing credibility

In companies where the strategic importance of the HR role has already been recognised, and its profile in the organisation successfully raised, it has often proved easier to import credibility from other functions than to confront the image problem directly.

For example, the training function at US electronics giant Motorola underwent a remarkable transformation in the 1980s as a result of the direct intervention of Bob Galvin, the company's chief executive officer (CEO). Galvin wanted to change the status of training to make it a strategic weapon to beat the Japanese competition. In deference to the low status of training within Motorola, he chose the top high-flyer in the company and offered him the job of head of the training function. The individual concerned turned it down, saying that it would damage his reputation. But Galvin convinced him that he could come back into the mainstream operation within a few years if he wanted to. He also offered to support him with investment and a concerted campaign in which he as CEO would personally champion training as a strategic priority.

Closer to home, car manufacturer Rover's creation of Rover Learning Business (RLB) represented a radical new approach to developing the company's people. The image of RLB was greatly strengthened within the Rover culture through some shrewd midwifery by the project team involved. They knew that a radical new approach was needed that went beyond the old training role. The time was right to do something, but they were not sure what it should be, or what it would look like.

A paper was circulated by Rover's personnel director, David Bower, about the 'Learning Organisation'. It helped trigger a breakthrough. Barrie Oxtoby, a senior member of the project team, felt that the quantum leap they needed was to transform the focus of the training role from one primarily concerned with teaching to one of facilitating learning. The idea of Rover Learning Business was conceived. Bower agreed that it was the right way forward and supported Oxtoby in marketing the concept to the organisation. Bower explains how they did it: 'We picked influential people and opinion formers inside Rover, including people who can be difficult. We knew that if we could identify and convince the right people and get them to sign on to it, we'd be able to swing it. In this way we began to bring RLB to life.'

When RLB was formally launched in May 1990, it achieved another significant coup by persuading Sir Graham Day (then chairman and chief executive of the Rover Group) to be its non-executive chairman. This ensured it a high profile both at board level and in the Rover organisation as a whole. But at the same time, if it was to be taken seriously within the company, it was important that it should have a degree of independence from the rest of the group. It had to be seen to stand on its own two feet and to manage its affairs efficiently. This was achieved by giving it the status of a business in its own right. This image was greatly strengthened by appointing Fred Coultas, a hardened line manager with a respected track record which included strategically vital new model launches, as its first managing director.

A cursory examination of its structure, however, reveals how closely RLB's architects intended it to reflect the priorities of the group as a whole. Its constitutional arrangements include some important checks and balances to optimise its impact on the Rover culture and to ensure that it continues to have a high profile within the company. For example, the executive committee – to whom the RLB core team reports each month – is deliberately made up of key Rover people, who constantly want to know what RLB is doing for Rover. This creates a positive pressure on Fred Coultas and his team to satisfy their demands. At the same time, a structured board of governors gives RLB a point of contact with the outside world which provides it with a constant input of fresh ideas.

And while personnel director David Bower agrees that it is difficult to assess the impact of RLB in promoting a learning culture at Rover, he points out that it is something the company takes very seriously. 'We have a number of hard input personnel measures that we apply in this area,' he says. 'For instance, we measure involvement by looking at things like participation in the company's employee suggestion scheme – which is up markedly. We also have measures for learning and development and resourcing and retention, and absenteeism. In this way, we continue to weave the web between personal development and benefits to the company in the future. The bottom line of RLB, after all, is to benefit the Rover Group.'

In both of these examples – Rover and Motorola – in order to raise the status of HR activities, it was simpler to put a non-HR manager in charge than to promote someone from within the function. Inspired as both were as solutions to the HR image problem, these examples underline the difficulties HR faces in overcoming its poor professional image.

If it is to be successful, any initiative to raise the profile of HR must take account of the current image of the function within the culture of the organisation. To a certain extent, too, the room for manoeuvre enjoyed by individual HR practitioners will also be tied to the overall standing of the function in the organisation. The more hostile the culture, the more difficult it will be for HR practitioners to introduce new ideas, products or services. It follows, therefore, that to stand a realistic chance of success, any strategy to market HR internally should start with a realistic evaluation of how it is currently viewed by its clients and customers.

It is important to realise, too, that while in some cases HR may receive credit just for trying to be more customer-oriented, the benefits of an HR marketing strategy must be carefully weighed against the dangers of failing to deliver what is promised. Such a failure could easily do more damage than good to the image of the function. We strongly recommend, therefore, that the more cynical the internal culture is towards HR, the more cautious the function should be about raising its profile initially. Occasionally, however, a unique opportunity invites a bold marketing foray by HR. The best scenarios are ones that offer a win-win situation.

Jerry Hallier, a lecturer in human resources management at Stirling University's School of Management, explains a fundamental problem for most HR departments and discusses how one HR function used a win-win marketing opportunity to gain credibility. 'The question for many senior HR practitioners,' he says, 'is how you get HR initiatives onto the strategic agenda in the first place, when so much of what is discussed at board level is determined by financial criteria. The answer for the HR department in a medium-sized engineering company came through identifying and solving a major strategic issue.'

The company concerned faced a serious skills mix problem. In particular, it was having difficulty recruiting enough people with the right computing skills to meet its requirements. There was stiff competition, too, from rival companies bidding for the same skills. As a result, the company was spending large amounts of money on recruitment in a limited skills pool. At the same time it was overstaffed in other areas and was forced to make redundancies across a range of skill areas, including people with technical skills no longer required for the business; and clerical and non-technical staff.

In managing the redundancy programme the HR function recognised a strategic opportunity. After careful consideration, it proposed a radical break with the company's existing recruitment practices by trying to redeploy redundant staff in the technical roles the company was competing in the job market to fill. It was a calculated risk that owed much of its success to careful marketing and high professional competence in the area of psychometric testing. The HR function anticipated correctly that line managers would resist the move in the belief that non-technical staff lacked the aptitudes required to train them in a new technical role. To overcome this objection, HR proposed that those facing redundancy who so desired be offered the opportunity to be assessed using specialised aptitude tests for software technicians which the company hadn't used before. HR's competence in selecting these tests was critical to the success of the initiative.

HR managers sold the idea to the managing director by pointing out that the cost of conducting such tests would be small, while at the same time the effect on the morale of remaining employees would be high. In other words, they presented the managing director with a win-win scenario which convinced him to let them try.

As they had predicted, the take-up among those facing redundancy was very high. Most important of all, however, a large number of those tested scored well in the psychometric tests. Although specialised training was required to give them the skills necessary to move into technical roles, the cost was considerably lower than the costs of recruiting skilled staff from outside. The redeployed staff subsequently moved into technical departments and did very well.

The success of the initiative and the competence demonstrated by the HR department enabled it to make the case that rather than fight with competitors for skilled staff, by widening the recruitment net the company could largely overcome its skills shortages problems in other divisions, too. In effect, HR had demonstrated a way to increase the size of the labour pool by including its own non-technical staff.

As Hallier points out, the success of the HR department's approach in this example resulted from the following key factors:

- The solution provided by HR represented a transferrable benefit. (Its approach to the redundancy programme had important strategic applications which offered a way forward for other parts of the business.) It was a classic case of taking two threats and using them to create an opportunity. It impressed senior management because it offered a strategic solution that could be applied else-where in the company. The result was a radical change to recruitment practices not just in the areas affected by the skills shortfall and the redundancy programme, but right across the company.

- It demonstrated that the expertise of HR is relevant to strategic issues.
- The risk to HR was minimised because senior managers were presented with a win-win scenario.
- The cost of the experiment was very low, so the cost of failure to HR's standing was minimal.
- It addressed an issue of great strategic importance to the business.
- It proved that HR could actually solve strategic problems.
- HR's heightened credibility in the area of psychometric testing also raised the professional standing of the function up a notch in the eyes of the organisation – enabling HR to introduce more rigorous approaches to the recruitment of senior managers.

The status of HR was dramatically improved as a consequence. Senior HR managers are now included at the front end of strategy formulation. They are able to influence how strategic issues are looked at in the boardroom.

For most HR functions, however, it is far better to start by tackling a relatively small issue that they know irritates line managers and to wait until the improvement is secure before advertising it, than to announce that you are going to set the world to rights and fail. Otherwise, unless the ground has been carefully prepared, the cynicism and disbelief of internal customers may itself be a major factor in making an initiative fail.

Building an image as a professional resource

Professionalising the HR function will have an important impact on its image and positioning in the internal market. A number of factors suggest that HR departments that fail to cultivate a professional, rather than a simply administrative, image risk becoming obsolete.

According to Jerry Saville, HR manager at Shell International, the key to professionalising the HR role lies in recognising its new role:

> HR was very defensive a few years ago. It suffered from a lack of confidence in itself, especially as the unions became weaker and the industrial relations role became less important in the early 1980s. HR questioned what it was there for. But at Shell we are now past that crisis of confidence. We analyse HR in terms of competencies needed. We are very aware of the need to establish the professionalism of the HR function within the organisation. Professionalism must be based on a clear career structure within HR. So a 30-year-old who's covered employment issues and training but done no development work must be given an opportunity to gain the necessary experience in that area.
>
> It's easier for a large company like Shell to achieve this. But all HR departments must be aware of the dangers of not having professional standards. If, for example, there is a tendency to try to dump failed line managers in HR, as HR professionals we must resist such moves.

The trend among organisations to outsource administrative tasks such as payroll, facilities management and recruitment means that HR must demonstrate new competencies. At the same time, this change has been accompanied in many organisations by moves to transfer traditional personnel responsibilities to line managers. As a consequence, there has been a shift in the skills base required by personnel functions, away from clerical skills and routine personnel tasks. These developments have led to a significant shift in the focus of HR. In many organisations, the role of today's HR practitioner is much more that of a specialist adviser, or internal consultant, whose main focus is to support line managers through professional interventions.

Recognising these changes, the IPM, in consultation with other professional bodies, looked at ways to support its members by introducing new professional qualifications for personnel practitioners. The creation of the IPM Professional Management Foundation Programme (PMFP), for example, enabled HR functions to raise the business awareness of staff wishing to enter the personnel profession. The PMFP, which is the first stage of the Institute's Professional Education Scheme (PES), is a broad-based management programme designed to develop an understanding of general management principles and key skills as a foundation for further professional development. The three areas of management practice covered are: management of people, management in context and management of systems.

It is no accident that these moves to upgrade the skills base of the profession coincide with a growing awareness among HR professionals that they need to find ways to justify their role within the businesses they serve. If they are no longer to be viewed as pen-pushing administrators – and therefore expendable – they must demonstrate that their specialist skills and 'professionalism' contribute to the business.

A bottom-up approach is the logical way to upgrade the HR skills base. In this context the IPM's Certificate of Personnel Practice is another useful addition. But there is a pressing need now to build on the professionalism of practitioners at all levels. In part, this should come from an ongoing review of personnel qualifications. The IPM's Continuous Improvement Scheme, which requires HR professionals to demonstrate that they are keeping abreast of changes, is an important development in this area. But it must also be driven by individual HR functions presenting a more professional face to the organisations in which they operate. Those HR functions which address the issue will not only be doing the profession as a whole a favour, but will improve their own standing with other functions in their organisation. The aim must be to make professionalism synonymous with the HR brand.

Typically, the professionalising of HR will include a switch away from its traditional, largely clerical, role towards one with greater emphasis on managing specialist know-how. Over time, the characteristics of the professional HR practitioner can be expected to undergo a shift from:

Administrator	to	internal consultant
Passive	to	proactive

Problem solver	to	solution facilitator
Information hoarder	to	information provider
Maker of rules/punisher	to	educator
Strategy follower	to	strategic thinker.

The HR function at Motorola's Land Mobile Products Sector has already gone some way towards redesigning its professional role. It characterised the transformation required in terms of a move from the old role of personnel as 'the functional expert' to the future role of HR as 'the unblocker'. Its approach involved defining and contrasting a number of past and future characteristics, including the following:

Past role of personnel

- hiring and firing
- training
- policies and procedures
- risk avoidance
- recruitment

Future role of HR

- organisational intervention
- consulting skills
- management of ambiguity
- removal of punishment/creation of trust
- acceptance, but management of inconsistency
- identifying and managing risk
- integrated approach
- facilitating personnel skills.

In doing so it signalled a clear change of values to its internal clients and customers.

Personal impact and visibility

The other side of the professionalism coin is the personal integrity and standards that individuals bring to the job. The

ITEM survey shows that the credibility and standing of the HR function with line managers is closely related to their perception of the HR professionals in charge. There is a great need among HR practitioners, especially those at a senior level, to realise that the impact they have as individuals is critical to the brand image of the function as a whole. We have mentioned the role that 'HR ambassadors' from other functions can play in marketing HR. HR staff themselves are automatically ambassadors for the function. Yet our research shows that this role is all too often poorly served, underestimated or simply neglected by senior HR managers.

In the ITEM survey, HR professionals identified as 'poor communicators', or 'lacking in personal communications skills' were singled out by line managers as a strong negative influence on their perception of the HR function. In one extreme case the HR director was seen as 'insensitive' and his 'heavy-handed' treatment of staff had clearly alienated line managers, who, as a result, were reluctant to involve the personnel department in staff problems requiring 'a sympathetic approach'. One manager reported that the HR director's attitude towards a pregnant employee over maternity leave made her feel like a 'parasite on the company' for wanting to leave and then return to her job. The line manager concerned understandably felt the need to protect staff from the HR director from then on. Elsewhere in the same company, the credibility of the HR function as a whole appeared to have been undermined by the HR director's actions, making line management resistant to the implementation of HR policies. At the other end of the spectrum, HR professionals held in high esteem by line managers were frequently described as 'approachable' and 'easy to talk to' and were perceived to have raised the overall credibility of the HR department.

Other comments included:

– The positive impact HR has on my job is in part the result of the personalities of personnel staff. The line manager role can be very lonely. I can't always discuss problems with other managers, but I find I can bounce ideas off the people in personnel who have the experience to guide me.

– HR here is like Fort Knox. There's a barrier of secretaries which makes it very difficult to get hold of them. I'd like to be able to just pop in and say: 'Hey I've got a problem can you help?', but at the moment I need an appointment.

– The evaluation process I found was one of aggression. The interrogation style of the individual from HR made it difficult to discuss things. Other line managers I've spoken to say the same.

– I was impressed when two senior personnel managers came around asking questions like, 'what aren't we doing for you that you need?'

– The individual personalities of the personnel staff must match the policies for the function to have credibility.

The long-term solution to this problem may be a heightened awareness of the significance of interpersonal skills for HR professionals, leading to the recruitment of the right people into the HR profession.

Getting to the top

Writing in the Jobs column of the *Financial Times* on 23 October 1991, Michael Dixon asked which of the following two candidates would be best suited to head the personnel function:

(A) who, although fully aware of business realities, is primarily a personnel professional with the characteristic attitudes and skills of that specialism highly developed by success in managing the various aspects of personnel work.

or

(B) who is primarily a business manager with the attitudes and skills typically developed by running operations in sales and production and so on, but whose knowledge of personnel issues is the rough and ready sort picked up in line management as distinct from the deep professional kind.

The point of the question, and indeed of the article, was to explore whether there are common traits among personnel specialists typified by candidate A that make them unsuitable for senior management posts.

The case against them making effective senior managers hinges here on the question of whether they have professional characteristics at odds with adding value to the bottom line, and if so whether it makes more sense for the top management team to 'buy in' specialist personnel expertise from outside as and when required. Dixon pointed to the findings of a study by Cambridge Recruitment Consultants which found that personnel professionals seen by their organisation as having senior management potential 'prefer thinking up solutions to actually pushing them through'. Worse, as well as being poor at taking tough action themselves, they find it hard to work harmoniously with colleagues of a more decisively active character.

This evidence – based on the results of the Cattel measure of personality traits and the Watson Glaser test of critical thinking – suggests that personnel professionals have a tendency to be poor at making tough decisions and acting swiftly and decisively.

Dixon himself was far from convinced. He pointed out that if personnel professionals are reluctant to take swingeing action in their field, 'the reason may be that their professional focus has taught them a realistic lesson which has not yet penetrated the tough skulls of many line managers – to wit, that it is unwise to treat people like so many machines'.

A 1990 study by Dr Stephen Harding of International Survey Research supports this observation. It found evidence of a trend for workforces in general to expect a higher degree of involvement in the running of their companies and more sensitive handling of personnel issues. This, as Dixon concludes, would seem to argue for more personnel involvement at the highest level, not less. Nevertheless, personnel professionals must demonstrate their effectiveness in senior management roles if they are to have a greater impact on strategy formulation.

HR professionals who reach senior positions in their organisations will be those who demonstrate a keen awareness of strategic issues and the enormous benefits of a more human approach to management. Over time, it is to be hoped that they will clear the obstacles to career progression from the HR function to senior management which in turn will help attract high-calibre managers to the HR function.

Checklist

- Are you clear about the difference between functional management and direction?
- Have you seized or created opportunities to gain breadth of management expertise?
- How does the quality of management in HR compare with the line?
- How well does HR understand the strategic business imperatives?
- Do you see your role as including helping to craft the business strategy?
- Do you have a professional development programme for HR staff that goes beyond functional expertise?

5

Gaining a Reputation for Quality

So far, we have tended to stress the difficulties of changing the HR image. But there are important opportunities open to HR practitioners involved in the implementation of total quality programmes which merit a chapter of their own. Broadly speaking, the opportunities fall into three categories:

- opportunities to reposition HR in a changed culture
- opportunities resulting from the role HR plays in driving quality implementation
- opportunities to apply quality management techniques to the HR function itself.

Repositioning HR in a changed culture

The implementation of a total quality strategy involves a major shift in an organisation's culture. This in itself is an opportunity for HR because the period of cultural flux that accompanies it means that many old assumptions are open to re-evaluation. Line managers trying to cope with what often seem to be threatening new situations are more likely to be receptive to HR practitioners who find ways to support them.

At Network SouthEast, for example, a series of cultural and organisational changes within British Rail provided the personnel function with an opportunity to reposition itself within the organisation. The traditional role of personnel at BR was composed of two elements: managing the trade union bargaining machinery through a process of institutionalised collective bargaining; and administration of a highly complex bureaucracy which included payroll, terms and conditions, shift patterns and overtime.

According to Bernard Williams, personnel director at Network SouthEast: 'In the eyes of most BR managers, personnel was characterised by stopping things rather than enabling them to happen. Because of its role of policing employees, it was seen as the function that liked to say no.'

By 1990, however, radical changes within BR meant that the role of personnel had to change. Two developments in particular meant that the organisation's culture was being redefined. The first involved the formation of a number of separate businesses including Network SouthEast and Intercity – which had formerly existed as marketing and planning vehicles, with no real independence or assets of their own. The move reflected BR's need to shift away from its production focus to become more business-oriented.

This change was accompanied by a total quality initiative which sought to establish:

- customer focus
- customer standards
- devolution of authority to local managers.

In the background, too, was the need to get the component parts of BR ready for privatisation.

At Network SouthEast the total quality management (TQM) programme was driven from the centre by a total quality function established specifically to implement and sustain it. The task facing the HR function was to reposition itself for a changed role in the emerging culture. It had to move from its old role of managing the status quo to a new one that would be characterised by interventions concerned with people-development issues. But many of the personnel managers who would have to support line managers and act as change agents at the nine newly created Network South-East profit centres were steeped in old culture and therefore relatively ill equipped for their new role. The key to managing the change was to work with the top managers at the profit centres to raise their expectations of what an HR function could deliver. However, many of them were relatively young managers thrust into challenging jobs, and they too were still adjusting to the new culture. However, they soon warmed to the task.

In line with the break-up of the organisation into separate

businesses, the collective bargaining machinery had to be renegotiated. The new bargaining procedures reinforced the devolution of power and local empowerment by placing responsibility for reaching agreements with local managers. These managers could no longer pass the problem up. Localised personnel staff and line managers had to learn to do 'deals'. To support them in their new role, line managers received training and briefing packs from the HR function. This significantly changed the positioning of local personnel staff.

At the same time, there was a change of focus with the new culture moving away from viewing HR in terms of inputs into people, towards outputs from them. The aim was to switch to a competency-based approach. Behind the change lay the idea that people must know the standard of service they were expected to provide, must be trained to deliver it and must then be assessed on their performance. This has led to the implementation of standards-based training.

The need to develop an effective programme to achieve the new focus led to pioneering work with the Management Charter Initiative (MCI) piloting standards-based training. Training had previously been centred on limited task-specific skills such as driving a train, rather than encompassing the sorts of attitudes and behaviours required to satisfy customers. The new approach, and the involvement at the cutting edge of training development, have played a significant part in repositioning HR within the organisation's culture.

Says Network SouthEast's Bernard Williams: 'There is no beginning or end to the process of change we're experiencing. But there is a definite movement in perception. The switch to competency-based training is the key to repositioning HR here.'

In another case, Shepherd Construction saw the Investors in People (IIP) initiative, which was launched jointly by the CBI, the Employment Department and Training and Enterprise Councils, as an opportunity to reinforce its long-standing commitment to training. IIP fitted well with the people side of the company's own quality programme, called

81

'Total Excellence'. It also provided a focus for the company's 1,400 employees to support the goals of the HR function.

Peter Blackburn, the company's training manager, acknowledges that the culture of the company, which is highly supportive of the HR function, and the personal commitment of the senior management were critical factors in the decision to raise the profile of HR by going for IIP recognition. In addition, he says: 'Paul Shepherd, the chairman and managing director, gave an oblique lead by distributing materials on the initiative to managers. It also had a very good fit with our culture and what we were trying to achieve.'

Although not directly represented at board level, the HR function is fortunate to be operating within a culture that recognises its contribution as an integral part of the business strategy. As a consequence, the head of the HR function is involved in strategy formulation and was able to convince senior managers to put their weight behind the IIP initiative.

Every employee received a letter from Paul Shepherd, outlining his personal commitment to the IIP initiative and spelling out its importance to the strategic role of HR within the company. 'I see our commitment as an "Investor in People" as being an important part of the company's aim to improve standards throughout the business,' he wrote. 'In a highly competitive market, our success in attaining this goal depends upon the combined efforts of all employees, and I hope you will feel that the latest initiative . . . will be a significant move in the ongoing development of the business.'

Peter Blackburn explains the effect the backing from top management had: 'When Paul Shepherd signed a pledge on behalf of the company to become an Investor in People, it was a public endorsement of all our people and the HR department in particular. It automatically raised our profile. We knew we had to deliver and everyone in the company, managers and staff alike, was completely committed to supporting the HR department to make the initiative a success.'

Shepherd Construction achieved IIP status in just a few months – an achievement which is all the more remarkable for a company operating in the recession-hit construction industry. Peter Blackburn puts the success of the initiative down to a combination of the professionalism of the HR staff and the enthusiasm of everyone in the company.

But the beauty of the IIP initiative for the training function was threefold. Not only was it an excellent vehicle to raise the status of HR internally, but it gave the HR function a platform which according to Peter Blackburn allowed it 'to put the broad goals of the company across to our people'. In addition, it offered a way to gain internal and external recognition for the company's long-term commitment to training.

Driving quality

In many organisations HR has been instrumental in implementing the change programmes required to bring about the cultural shift to total quality. This involvement with a major component of the organisation's strategy is in itself significant. The move to TQM is a high-profile one, and one that, if it is to be successful, must have the whole-hearted support of top management. As such, it provides HR with an excellent chance to demonstrate its value to the business. Quality programmes carry a great deal of weight within the organisation. HR practitioners should capitalise on this by actively marketing their role as change initiators or change facilitators. Where change programmes are successful, the standing of HR will automatically increase, providing an ideal opportunity to reposition the HR brand.

A recent study commissioned by the IPM[1] looked at the part played by the personnel function in organisations seeking to achieve quality management. The study, which was in three parts including a questionnaire sent to organisations in the UK, a telephone survey of personnel managers throughout mainland Europe and the USA, and an in-depth case-study analysis of 15 organisations, set out to assess the contribution of personnel professionals to the practice of quality management, and to suggest ways in which that contribution could be extended.

Its authors, Angela Baron from the IPM and Mick Marchington, Barrie Dale and Adrian Wilkinson from the University of Manchester Institute of Science and Technology (UMIST), found that the role of personnel in quality programmes varies greatly. But their findings suggest a much more central role for personnel than earlier studies show. Writing in *Personnel Management*[2] the UMIST team summarised the findings of the survey as follows:

- Three-quarters of UK organisations implementing quality initiatives involve their HR people in some way, although their role is often limited to operational activity and in particular training issues.
- When HR people are involved at the strategic level, the perspective of the quality management initiative tends to be broader and more long-term.
- There are significant differences between the approaches used by the private and public sectors, with the public sector placing more emphasis on people and their contribution to delivering quality aims and objectives.
- There is some indication that involvement in quality is resulting in changes in the way personnel departments operate. These changes are generally characterised by a more customer-focused approach to the delivery of HR services.
- Over 80 per cent of the organisations in the survey sample had experienced problems in implementing quality, which were associated with people. The problems were mainly associated with generating acceptance of, and commitment to, the aims of quality.
- Training and personnel policies to support quality aims and objectives were seen by the majority of respondents as the areas in which HR could have most impact on quality.
- In America there are indications that HR issues and policies are generally more integrated into business, and the involvement of HR practitioners appears to be stronger at all levels than in the UK.
- American-owned companies appear more likely to involve HR in quality at a strategic level.

While these findings represent something of a mixed bag of good and not so good news for UK personnel practitioners, another part of the study shows that when it comes to responsibility for overseeing quality – be it via a quality steering committee, or by other means – HR often plays an important part. The department or person responsible for quality varied considerably across the sample, but in four cases out of the 15, the HR function played a major role: at Gefco, a French freight forwarding company, and at Gould Electronics, quality and HR had been combined in the same function/person; at Peterborough Priority Services (an NHS trust which is now part of North West Anglia Priority Services) quality reported to the HR function; and at Racal Data Networks the HR and quality functions had jointly developed quality management.

Most of the organisations in the study had set up a dedicated committee for overseeing quality management. In most cases, too, the quality committee was chaired by the managing director or equivalent. Personnel professionals had a place on most of these TQM steering committees or quality councils.

The study characterised HR involvement in quality programmes in terms of four distinct roles; the first and second relate primarily to the operations level, while the third and fourth are strategic roles.

- *Facilitator* – this role was apparent in all the cases. It typically involves the HR function providing hands-on support for line managers. It could be derived from requests from line managers for help with some aspect of quality management such as providing training courses, or organising a roadshow or newsletter to publicise achievements. In many respects this role is indistinguishable from the normal day-to-day activities that line managers expect from HR to ensure quality management is effective. At Bedfordshire County Council, for example, the personnel department organised a leaflet introducing the council's new management style, and distributed a statement of the organisation's new values to all employees.

- *Internal contractor* – this role is characterised by an attempt by personnel to set and publicise targets or standards for the delivery of HR services to internal clients and customers. For example, the software company Praxis achieved BS 5750 series registration in 1986. The company's HR function had produced its own simple quality targets after talking to HR customers. HR identified ten areas of personnel products, ranging from recruitment through to pay and performance review. In each case the customers were named and the time by which the service would be provided was stated. So, for example, offers and contracts were to be provided to line managers within 24 hours of request.
- *Change agent* – this role is both strategic and high profile. It might involve the HR function being responsible for helping to drive quality management or playing a leading part in a culture-change programme which paves the way for quality management. In this situation, quality management is seen as synonymous with change and HR is defined (or manages to define itself) as the function best able to lead the change process. For example, at Ilford, part of the Imaging Products Division of US-owned International Paper, it was widely recognised that HR has played a major role in developing TQM by creating the structure and culture within which TQM was possible.

  At Peterborough Priority Services, quality co-ordinator Diane Driver reports to the director of HR and quality, Jan Bailey, and for years the personnel function has been leading the way with new initiatives. For example, before the organisation implemented its own (pre-government) patients' charter, Bob Ricketts, personnel director of the old health authority, had introduced an employee charter. Jan Bailey currently chairs the organisation's quality forum, and plays a leading role on other quality bodies.
- *Hidden persuader* – this role is at a strategic level, but is not particularly prominent within the organisation. So, although the HR contribution is regarded highly by the managing director or equivalent, it is much less visible to other managers and employees. In one case, for example, at Racal Data Networks, the HR function was chosen to

help the quality department develop quality management because it was viewed as neutral and able to take an overview of the change process without pursuing its own departmental agenda to the detriment of the organisation as a whole.

In the role of hidden persuader, HR is frequently used as a sounding board for new ideas and is often consulted prior to wider discussion within the company.

Marchington, Dale and Wilkinson conclude that personnel and HR departments are playing 'a sizeable role' in quality management initiatives. They acknowledge, however, that there is no simple prescription for all personnel managers to follow in order to enhance their contribution and raise their profile. 'Much,' they say, 'depends on the kind of organisation in which personnel is operating, its status and influence, and the resources at its disposal. But there are a number of phases at which the personnel function can make a contribution to quality management.' Among these they suggest:

- shaping initiatives at the formulation phase, through actions such as the design and delivery of management development courses or synthesising reports from other organisations with experience of quality management
- introducing initiatives by helping to ensure that they are implemented correctly, through actions such as the training and coaching of facilitators or designing communications events to publicise quality management
- reinforcing initiatives so as to maintain continuous improvement, through actions such as the redesign of appraisal procedures to include quality criteria or the preparation of special quality management newsletters
- reviewing initiatives to evaluate progress, through actions such as the preparation of an annual TQM report or by carrying out employee attitude surveys on a regular basis
- applying quality management principles to the personnel function itself to increase its effectiveness and improve its credibility.

The HR function at British Airways recognised in the late

1980s that it could no longer afford to launch initiatives on its own. To achieve any significant impact on the organisation, HR had to build line management closely into the planning and decision-making process. In developing an approach to company-wide TQM, it carried out extensive research among customers and staff in general and amongst line managers in particular. In a series of focus groups, the top 70 managers were quizzed, says HR general manager Chris Byron, 'on what they felt were the key domains to deliver customer service and to deliver their business goals'.

As a result of these discussions, BA set up a quality board to steer and co-ordinate the progress of quality initiatives across the company. This board included a cross-section of top management. This type of high-level, multi-disciplinary group was established as a model for driving change through HR, explains Byron. 'We recognised that, on a number of key HR specialisms, we needed the buy-in of line managers. So we created a series of cross-functional groups for both steering and implementation. I can't think of any recent HR intervention that has come entirely from within HR. They have all been shaped with the involvement of line managers.'

One of the first was to create an HR strategy board, chaired by the CEO and involving other directors. Reporting to this are a number of specialist groups, including:

- The executive academy, which manages succession planning for the top 150 or so managers
- The management academy, which assesses external training and development courses (such as MBAs) for senior managers
- The compensation group, which sets pay and reward policies
- The manpower group, which looks at skills requirements for the company.

These can create their own sub-groups, if needed. For example, a working party on management styles reports to the management academy.

In each case, the specialist HR staff present papers and recommendations to the appropriate board. The recommendations themselves are frequently developed by teams consisting of the HR specialists and line staff seconded by the relevant member of the board.

This growing understanding and sharing of objectives between HR and line managers has been reinforced by a recruitment policy that seeks line-management experience in new HR appointments.

Applying quality management to the HR function

The third kind of opportunity for HR is from applying quality management techniques to enhance its own processes. Because the new TQM culture recognises quality as its guiding light, it will respond to an HR function that speaks the same language. Since most of these organisations will either have gone through, or be going through, the pain of achieving BS 5750 accreditation or the equivalent, they will respect an HR function that exposes itself to the same discipline, particularly since it is only now that service functions such as IT and HR are starting to get to grips with how the quality concept applies to them.

The reasons why quality management has been slow to take hold in HR departments are the usual ones of finding meaningful performance indicators to measure. Service functions simply do not lend themselves to measurement in quite the same way as manufacturing output or compliance with a customer's specifications. Frequently, service organisations are more about creating intangible benefits such as a sense of confidence or satisfaction with the way something was handled or a problem was solved. Often, too, such intangible benefits cannot be easily explained even by the recipients. All of which makes the application of quality to HR problematic.

It is all very well to say, 'We want to get non-compliance of the steel bolts we produce down to 1 in 10,000.' But it is not so easy to know how to make that sort of approach stick when you are talking about the non-compliance of individual employees' experiences on a given training course. For one thing, each person will start out on a training course with different expectations. In fact, it is because HR deals with that most complex and non-homogeneous of material, the human mind, that the use of quality approaches is more difficult.

The fact remains however that an HR function that sets itself the target of becoming BS 5750 accredited, and then once it achieves its goal uses that accreditation as part of its brand image, can do much to boost its standing with other functions. For example, the computer company ICL gained BS 5750 accreditation in the late 1980s. Personnel was not the driver of the quality initiative but was involved from the start. As the company introduced what quality manager Dave Fawcett describes as a 'wall-to-wall' approach to quality, the personnel department was treated no differently from any other function.

At ICL, the very nature of personnel is about key processes and standards and the department was pleasantly surprised to find that BS 5750 was not too difficult to achieve. Being at the core of business activities, Fawcett believes the personnel function benefited from the discipline of the standard. Personnel is now subject to annual internal audit visits from the quality department as well as visits from the British Standards Institute (BSI) which administers the quality registration process, just like all of the company's other departments. These visits ensure that continuous improvement of personnel processes is maintained.

It is important to realise, too, that becoming BS 5750 accredited is the natural route for external HR suppliers to take. By so doing they will greatly increase their chances of selling HR expertise to organisations where quality processes are already required of other external suppliers. The danger for the internal function lies in failing to recognise the enhanced brand image that such external HR suppliers will command with managers who speak the language of quality.

Checklist

- Is HR a driving force in TQM, or merely an implementer?
- Are you seeking to capitalise on experience with TQM to position HR as the driver of other major cultural change initiatives?
- Do you apply TQM principles to HR activities as a matter of course?

PART III
Changing Perceptions

6

Building Relationships

In the days when human resources was personnel and the main activities were industrial relations and salary and benefits, trust, where it existed at all, was seen as a weapon to gain compliance from the workforce. Industrial relations staff concentrated on developing close personal relationships with key employee representatives, in the hope of moderating demands and controlling dissent. Even where they were successful, the net result was usually a high degree of distrust among line managers, who – usually quite rightly – felt left out of the power play and undermined by personnel. Among the obvious and natural responses to this sense of powerlessness was to dump *all* people problems back on personnel.

Although the balance of power has now shifted away from the HR–employee axis and firmly into the hands of the line managers themselves, the relationship between line management and HR is frequently still tainted by the historical legacy of distrust. In such situations, trust does not evolve naturally, even though the memory of distrust fades. Negative stereotypes have been created in the perception of internal customers ('perfidious personnel' as one line manager expressed it) and these can only be overturned by a proactive approach to building relationships of trust. Some truisms apply here:

- Trust can only be built between individuals, not entities.
- Trust is much easier to destroy than to build.
- Trust takes time to develop – it is normally built out of numerous small transactions, rather than one large one.
- Trust is absolute – it is little use if line managers only trust some HR people, or only in some circumstances.
- Trust is a mixture of emotional and rational responses – with the emotional frequently predominating.

Given these truisms, it follows that the only sure way to build trust is to get close to the customer, continuously reinforcing positive aspects of HR. In essence, there are three components to professional trust:

- Trust in your integrity and goodwill.
- Trust that you share common objectives, or are open about conflicting objectives.
- Trust in your competence to do what you promise.

US psychologist Carl Rogers[1] specifies three critical requirements before trust can be established and cites a number of cases, such as the Camp David agreements, as examples. These requirements are:

- *Unconditional positive regard* – essentially this means accepting that the other person has a rational and/or valid reason for his or her views. It means suspending stereotype bias and the labels that accompany it. The HR professional can encourage this behaviour by demonstrating it him- or herself. For example, by using the jargon of the line department, rather than HR-speak, he or she can establish a willingness to take line managers on their own terms. Because behaviour breeds behaviour, reciprocal concessions from line managers are predictable.
- *Congruence* – this means being open and honest about your thoughts and feelings; in other words, not playing politics and not being manipulative. It means being able to state your fears and discuss them rationally.
- *Empathy* – this involves putting yourself in the other person's shoes, understanding his or her motivation and fears.

All three of these conditions apply to the HR–line manager relationship, both when conducting negotiations and in day-to-day transactions. By honestly examining how you approach the relationship, you can pinpoint where your attitudes and behaviours lead or reinforce lack of trust. Such insights will be helpful in approaching line managers with a view to changing their attitudes and behaviours.

Our survey[2] of relationships between HR and line managers revealed a high level of distrust on the part of the latter. Some of their more extreme comments included:

– The personnel director here has trodden on too many toes to be trusted with major initiatives. The attitude now is 'Oh no, not another idea from personnel.'

– The new man steamed in and started meddling in inappropriate areas like company car policy. He would have done better to have found his feet first, but instead he personally irritated and alienated a lot of people.

– Personnel succeeded in making one of my staff who needed maternity leave feel like a parasite on the company. I will never trust them with an employee again.

The problems, where they exist, are frequently deep-rooted. To overcome them, the HR function needs to adopt a coherent customer-centred process aimed at developing special relationships of trust with the key influencers/decision makers and general relationships of trust with the multitude of other customers and clients in the organisation.

Adopting the market-segmentation approach outlined in Chapter 2, the starting point is to define very precisely who the key market segments are. Typically, there will be four:

- top management
- key line managers
- line managers in general
- employees in general.

You may wish to add a fifth and/or sixth:

- people in the department
- suppliers to the department.

Each segment has different requirements and will have different barriers to achieving relationships of trust with HR. For top management and key line managers, it pays to adopt a 'key account' approach. Start by defining who are the principal individuals or teams whose goodwill and regard you need most. Do you know what motivates them – both overtly and covertly?

Key account management is effectively an approach to targeting marketing efforts on the most important customers. It can be characterised as involving two Cs and two Ps – **credibility, creativity, partnership** and **penetration**.

Credibility

Credibility is about establishing reputations. It cannot easily be developed by advertising or promotion. Rather, the critical vehicles are direct personal experience and word of mouth. Both help to do one of three things: create a perception where none existed before; reinforce a perception; or change a perception. The more a perception is based on stereotypes, the harder it is to change.

In his book *'Relationship Marketing'*, Regis McKenna[3] maintains that credibility begins with strong positioning. We can interpret this as being very clear about what the HR department offers and what it is there is to do for the company and for the key internal customers; in other words what we stand for.

Whether it pays to be specific and open about HR's positioning depends on where you are. If the positioning is close to reality and will be borne out by direct personal experience and thus by word of mouth, then advertising – through articles in the company newspaper, in periodicals from HR to line management or through presentations to line managers – will act as a powerful reinforcement. If the desired positioning and the reality are miles apart, then it is best to get the HR house in order before launching any form of promotion. It would be rather like the TSB advertising campaign that emphasised how much the bank liked to say 'yes'. Every customer who was told 'No' was a potential negative ambassador.

At Kingfisher plc, for example, there was identified a business need to design and develop a coherent group-wide strategy for senior management development. It was essential that the new approach be seen to recognise and reflect the needs of the individual operating companies and not simply as a solution imposed from the centre.

A genuine sense of joint ownership was key to its success. Kingfisher's HR director Tony Ward knew the project was an important stepping stone to enhancing the strategic role of HR within the company.

To gain the commitment of senior management participants, he knew he had to sell the group concept to the businesses. To do so he had to get the managing directors of the operating companies to sign up to the plan, and personnel directors to share leadership of the concept.

The vision and philosophy to underpin the strategy was developed by the HR team from the centre in conjunction with HR managers from the operating companies. The intended solution was then approved and endorsed by the group senior executives – group directors and managing directors from the main operating companies.

Implementation involved the creation of a number of project teams which were intentionally drawn from across the businesses and from a range of business functions. It was important to involve key people from all areas to build support for and consensus about the plan as it was rolled out. The project teams were facilitated by HR managers. The idea is that the project teams will develop and implement the various elements of the plan, which is seen as part organisational development and part personal development for participants.

At the same time, the process is being communicated widely to ensure maximum buy-in and involvement from all senior managers. As a result of the deft handling of the project, the management development process at Kingfisher is now cross-company, cross-functional and dynamic.

What positioning should we aim for?

In early 1993, ITEM was asked to looked at the positioning of the HR function in a major UK transport company. One of the results was a set of brand values, as. follows:

- strategic thinking – driven by HR
- HR professionalism
- close identity with customers
- piloting best management practice
- value awareness – driven by HR
- innovation – driven by HR
- rapid response
- global perspective (important for an international company).

These brand values could almost be generic, in that they define the ideal relationship between an HR function and its customers. A variation on these values may make a good starting point for developing a position for the service. Other considerations might be:

- how our values match against our capability to deliver
- how they match against the perception of us in our internal market
- how they match against the perception in our internal market of using external agencies in delivering the same services.

An effective service position will define – to HR staff initially, but ultimately to customers too – what the customer should feel during and after every transaction with HR. The objective is to create a relationship based on 'no surprises' for either party. Of course, it is possible to position HR against intended changes. However, middle managers in particular will at best suspend judgement and at worst dismiss such positioning as not credible unless there are already strong signs that you are well along the path towards achieving the quality of product and service you aim at.

Building credibility depends mainly on consistently exceeding expectations in transaction after transaction over a period. It can be helped, however, says McKenna,[4] by inference, reference and evidence.

Inference comes from the people with whom you associate. The higher their reputation, the more likely some of it is to rub off on you. 'If X supports this, it must be worthwhile.' Reputations can be built by inference in a variety of ways. Within the company, you can identify a target audience of managers who are highly regarded for their ability. Then you have to make a special effort to get close to them – and to be seen to do so. At British Airways, for example, HR has looked at ways of developing a network of champions among line managers to support the company's quality initiatives. HR would then involve these line managers closely in its thinking and decision-making processes, after using them as a sounding board for new ideas, and providing frequent opportunities for them to meet both HR and each other. At Rover Learning Business this approach was taken right to the very top of the company by persuading the then chairman of Rover Group Sir Graham Day to be a non-executive director of RLB. Credibility was also enhanced by the calibre of non-executives, including top academics and board directors from other leading companies.

Reference can be both positive and negative. It can occur spontaneously (one manager telling another about a good or bad experience) or deliberately (one manager asking another if he or she can recommend a good course or person to talk to). Pharmaceutical companies harness the power of reference by putting on short educational seminars attended by both users and non-users of their products. The success rate, in terms of changed opinions by their non-users, is often very high. The same basic approach can be used in reputation building among internal customers. The keys to success include:

- keeping the meetings relatively small (no more than 25–30 people) to maintain an atmosphere of intimacy and exchange of confidence
- having a genuine educational/informational reason for the event – it must not smell of a sales pitch
- ensuring high-quality facilitation
- maintaining a balance between believers and disbelievers
- being extremely careful not to make either believers or disbelievers feel manipulated.

Evidence helps build credibility, says McKenna, because 'success . . . reinforces itself'. HR's success in introducing new programmes of changes, in applying quality processes to its own activities and in helping some line managers achieve their objectives, all help to build up a case that it pays line managers to establish a good relationship with HR. Other ways of building evidence include:

- being sought out for help by other companies line managers will respect
- winning industry awards and accolades (HR professional

awards may have less impact among line managers who have a negative perception of HR in general!)
- the credible measurement of benefits from HR activities, expressed in line management terms (e.g. how a department improved its productivity as a result of training, not how satisfied employees were with the training programme).

All three building blocks of credibility – inference, reference and evidence – depend on achieving consistency. Mixed experience or mixed messages simply reinforce the perception of confusion and unreliability. To use inference effectively, HR must associate with corporate winners and avoid the losers. We have seen a number of cases where HR has chosen a manager as a champion, largely because he or she has time and interest. More often than not, such individuals have time because they have been put out to grass.

Reference requires consistency in the delivery of service promises – if not in exceeding customer promises – as does evidence.

McKenna's description of the drivers of product or service credibility misses out on at least one additional major driver when applied to internal markets – what we can call perceived professional competence. A survey carried out by consultants Young Samuel Chambers for the Personnel Standards Lead Body identified four basic competencies chief executives seek in the HR function. As described in the *Human Resources Management Yearbook 1993*,[5] these are:

- They insist that they need people who really understand the financial and market context of the business and can work familiarly with all the business concepts that any good general manager would use. Only if these people are truly business literate will they be able to make judgements about what is needed and fashion appropriate responses.
- They need someone who is able to 'read' the organisation and the individuals within it and to give honest feedback.

This, of course, requires not only considerable insight in understanding the complex nuances of individuals and of organisational communities, but also great courage and confidence in being able to give the bad news as well as the good, to show that the CEO's own behaviour may need to change, and to be willing to say the unsayable to people in a skilled and acceptable way without damaging them.

- They need help in understanding and marshalling the processes – managerial, relational and conceptual – which will bring about a new way of creating and implementing strategy. They are disillusioned with the large reports from corporate planners and from strategy boutiques which are full of brilliant analysis and worthy intent but which remain as aspiration rather than practical action. They want to work with those closest to the customer to understand what is possible within a broad strategic framework. They need someone to set up processes to ensure that the strategy–operational link is solidly there, informing organisational direction and guiding operational activity.

- They need help in developing the organisation, and in advising them of how to attract and keep good people and how to develop a really vibrant environment for working, which provides long-term satisfaction as well as delivering the highest-quality products and services to customers.

Creativity

Creativity refers to the degree to which the HR department is prepared to adapt its procedures and processes to meet the requirements of line-manager customers and its ability to come up with innovative solutions when required. The more that line managers feel HR is trying to solve their problems rather than its own, the easier it is to build trust.

Developing creativity in these circumstances is largely a matter of active listening, together with a willingness to start with the ideal solution and work back to the feasible (as opposed to the normal approach of starting with what we do now and seeing how we might adapt it if we have to).

Active listening is an essential prerequisite for understanding the concerns of a senior-level management audience. Our survey showed that this was a characteristic strongly approved of by senior line managers. A number of those interviewed said they were impressed by HR managers who used active-listening techniques. These include:

- writing down critical points
- asking probing questions
- paraphrasing ideas to check that they have understood the point being made
- challenging the ideas put forward (in a non-hostile, constructive way)
- intelligent use of open questions (ones that invite more information such as 'why?' and 'how?)' and closed questions (ones that invite a 'yes' or 'no' response)
- giving good feedback to reassure them that their needs are understood
- agreeing action points.

Partnership

Partnership in this context is about the ability to treat each key customer as a strategic alliance. This invariably requires changes in both behaviour and systems. It also requires the development of team-working skills both within HR and between HR and its key customers. At the other extreme from partnership relationships are adversarial ones. Highlighting the differences between the two is a good way to focus on the sorts of behaviours required to build positive relationships with customers.

Adversarial relationships are characterised by interactions where:

- both sides aim to beat the other – prioritising short-term gain at the expense of the other side
- customers are unwilling to share long-term plans
- both sides pay lip-service to partnership.

True partnership relationships on the other hand are typified by interactions where:

- both parties aim for win-win relationships which serve the long-term interests of both partners
- customers involve suppliers in developing new concepts
- both sides attach a high value to the partnership relationship.

At the Royal Dutch Shell Group of companies the Group HR function places a great deal of emphasis on its partnership role in management development. The corporate HR function works within a matrix which relates between regions, operating companies and different sectors of the business. It recognises that its main purpose in existing at the corporate level is to emphasise the corporate need. From that the following statement was derived:

Human Resource development promotes the long-term continuity of the Group through resourcing and development of management and professional staff.

According to HR manager Jerry Saville, the word 'promotes' is important. It indicates 'working with', but not actually 'deciding'. The words 'long-term' and 'continuity' are also significant particularly at a time when there is a lot of short-term pressure on the bottom line and many line managers are thinking little if any further ahead than tomorrow.

Another key part of the Shell approach is the way that management development is closely tied to the business philosophy. The benefits of an international management development system can be represented as follows:

- *Global insights at senior levels*. The ultimate aim is to get into the boardroom the people who have had the widest and the best experience that a manager could possibly have in a lifetime. There is, therefore, an aim in the system of selecting and filtering; that aim is to get those people up to the top, running the company on a global basis.

- *Top management involvement.* Related to the previous point is the importance of getting the involvement of top management itself. Top management must be involved and must get to know the people who are, in essence, their resource.
- *Testing high-potential staff.* A vital element of development is the challenge of suddenly dropping someone in at the deep end. Most people have had the experience of taking over from someone else; there comes a day when you are actually behind the desk doing their job. The phone rings and for the first time you are answering it as the person doing that job. It is at this point, after all the briefing and reading of files, that you actually begin learning very fast. Survival and building on experience of this type gives an individual tremendous self-confidence and sends a signal to the organisation that they can survive under these conditions.
- *Revolution within evolution.* Shell is not the sort of organisation that could be knocked flat and rebuilt quickly. The Group has evolved and changed a great deal in the last 25 to 30 years. Within that evolution there have been individual revolutions with parts of the business being turned around by sending in new people. The company does not believe in status quo and expects considerable commercial benefits from the way its human resources are managed.
- *Cultural and functional interchange and career stimulation.* The benefits of these are widely recognised within the company, which has a larger number of ex-pats than any other multinational company (more than 5,500 in 1993). To maintain the momentum, however, requires renewal and revitalisation for people in this sort of activity.
- *Promoting and effecting cohesion.* Cohesion comes from the shared values resulting from people moving around the world. This helps the process of proper delegation at the local level, while retaining a common understanding of what the business is all about. It is the corporate glue which holds the organisation together.

Adversarial relationships breed:

- suspicion
- combat
- information guarding
- customers who define their requirements without consulting HR
- characterisation of HR offerings as 'off the peg'
- customers who question the quality of HR products and services.

Partnership relationships breed:

- mutual trust
- teamwork
- open communication and sharing of information
- sharing of strategy to arrive at joint solutions
- customers open to HR solutions tailored to their specific requirements
- a trust in HR to deliver quality products and services.

Building partnership relationships usually starts by asking internal customers if they would be willing to invest the time and effort needed. You can emphasise the benefits to the customer (more rapid, effective responses because you understand their objectives, both overt and covert; fewer problems and errors; reduced problems; and so on) to persuade them at least to give it a try. Having gained an initial commitment, you will then need to deliver some swift, visible results. By testing out the key problems within the customer–supplier relationship, you can identify one or two priorities. These should be:

- capable of rapid resolution/improvement
- readily apparent to the customer (and if possible to his or her customers and colleagues).

Partnership is then reinforced by regular, frank meetings. You may have to set the example, perhaps by being rather more open about shortcomings than would normally be the case. However, because 'behaviour breeds behaviour', your openness and willingness to collaborate will eventually bear fruit. The greatest danger is that you will become discouraged and give up too early. Remember, you are participating in a significant culture change, and that will always require time and the strength to overcome frequent setbacks.

Penetration

Partnership is not just a one-dimensional activity. Whatever the relationship between principals, effectiveness derives from a host of interactions with a variety of people in the line organisation. No matter what agreement is reached between the HR director and the senior line manager responsible for a functional area, the ability to build on that relationship depends on the relationships other HR staff establish with a range of key influencers in the line organisation. As part of the HR planning process you should:

- Develop an 'account profile' of each key customer, describing not only the department's current strategy, but who is responsible for carrying out each major element; it may also include an analysis of likely needs for HR support (opportunities to market) and an assessment of the current perceptions of HR in that part of the organisation.
- Use good relationships on the ground to build a detailed and accurate picture of the decision-making process in that area of the company.
- Develop a systematic approach for influencing these key influencers in a manner that will not draw fire from the senior manager customer.

At the level of line managers and employees in general, it is often not practical to build special personal relationships. A different approach is needed, more akin to customer care. In essence, this means identifying the most important service factors to each major segment of this broad audience; setting standards and measuring performance against them; and communicating frequently and effectively. These processes are covered in Chapters 3 and 8 respectively.

The branding approach (covered in more detail in Chapter 7) provides a useful basis for building relationships across a broad front.

However, Jerry Saville, HR manager at the Royal Dutch Shell Group of companies, offers an important caveat:

> There is a danger in HR functions regarding themselves solely as a support function and becoming too subservient . . . HR was formerly regarded as a backroom activity. Now it must be seen as a function that adds value. It mustn't be a slave to line managers; rather, it must demonstrate that it has something to contribute.
>
> HR must be the custodian of certain standards. It might have to uphold the ethical climate on issues such as discrimination or disciplinary issues, for example. At times that might mean standing up to line managers to ensure that the correct procedures are followed. At the same time HR must be aware of the price its services cost to ensure the company is getting good value for its money.
>
> The relationship with line managers isn't one of a pure customer. But the idea of marketing is quite right. You've got to get close to line managers, but HR needs to be assertive in some of its roles.

Summary

Building a reputation that promotes trust takes time. However, being clear about *how* you want to position HR will help you deliver a consistent, coherent message. With time – and with the benefit of the positive word-of-mouth promotion that results from better relationships with top management and key influencers – a relationship of trust will develop with the vast majority of people in the organisation.

Checklist

* What is the level of trust between HR and line management? How do you know?

- What active steps are you taking to build trust?
- Do you have a clear set of HR values that will promote trust?
- Do you meet promises to customers consistently?
- Do you expect line managers to fit in with your procedures or do you expect to fit in with theirs?

Developing an HR Brand

Branding, as the term implies, means marking a product or service, or clusters of products or services, with a distinctive and easily recognisable sign. It is extremely valuable when building an HR marketing platform for the future.

The power of branding

According to Philip Kotler:[1] 'The power of a brand is demonstrated when a sufficient number of customers demand that brand and refuse a substitute even if the price is somewhat lower.'

In marketing terms, branding serves a number of useful purposes, including:

- differentiation in the marketplace
- high visibility
- image enhancement
- consistency of message
- creation of a sense of ownership among those involved with the brand
- product association
- reputation reinforcement
- continuity, because the brand has an intrinsic value, independent of particular product or service offerings

Taking these points individually, we can begin to see how branding can be used by HR functions to position themselves more effectively in the internal marketplace.

Differentiation in the marketplace

Like all functions, HR must find ways to demonstrate the contribution it makes to the business. To do so, it must ensure that what it does is distinguishable both from what other functions in the organisation do, and from what external suppliers offer. An HR department that has a high reputation for training might benefit from stamping its brand image on training materials. That way, no one in the organisation will make the mistake of thinking that training is provided by external suppliers or by another function. For example, we referred earlier to the training department at the Woolwich Building Society, which brands all materials it generates for internal consumption with its own logo. This ensures that the personnel brand is instantly recognisable within the company.

High visibility

We have already touched on the dangers and benefits of the HR function making itself highly visible, but visibility will be the key to raising its profile. The branding of high-profile activities is one way to ensure that HR gets the credit for successes to which it is entitled.

Image enhancement

The ITEM survey[2] shows that line managers are influenced in their opinion of HR by the professionalism and quality of its output. A well-managed HR brand gives the function a professional corporate identity. The simple use of an HR logo or letterhead, for example, means that materials emanating from HR have a 'crisp', professional feel to them.

Consistency of message

It is very important to the standing of HR that it be seen to speak with one voice. A strong brand image is the logical way to tie different parts of the HR portfolio together and communicate core brand values to customers and clients. The ITEM survey, for example, found that the HR function in one company sent contradictory messages and used different appraisal forms at different sites.

Until a few years ago, electrical retailer Comet had a confusing system of personnel policies and procedures. The grading in areas such as pay and conditions and company cars was inconsistent. With a background agenda of cutting costs, HR set about introducing consistent bandings. Aware that some people would lose out by the changes, the HR director was careful to segment his audience. Mindful that some of his peers (ie other directors) would also lose by the changes, they were handled on a one-to-one basis. Middle managers received briefing packs, which included materials to help them cascade information to other levels. All materials were branded with the Comet logo and the slogan 'Making it happen', devised by the HR function.

Creation of a sense of ownership

The effects of a strong brand image on employee morale and esteem can be considerable. One only has to look, for example, at the positive way British Airways employees responded to their branding as 'the world's favourite airline' to see the power of association with a professional image.

Another example comes from Pitman-Moore, where the entire HR staff from the European operation, including secretarial support, was brought together for a long weekend at an exclusive health spa for an extended brainstorming session. All members of the function were encouraged to take part in evaluating what HR priorities should be in the future, in the light of detailed market research among line managers. In addition, HR employees at all levels, from secretary up, outlined their vision for their current role in the function in five years' time. All those present then committed themselves to a vision for the HR function in the future and set themselves targets to achieve in the next few months to make that vision become a reality. So, for example, secretarial staff agreed that they would turn around certain administrative requests in 24 hours.

Product association

A strong brand image reassures customers that what is being provided is of a certain standard. Well managed, the brand becomes a hallmark of quality and credibility. If people have confidence in the HR brand, they will instantly recognise that any activity bearing that brand is of value. A strong brand image makes it much easier to launch new services and products.

Reputation reinforcement

Branding means that individual HR successes add to the reputation and standing of the function as a whole. So the successful implementation of a quality programme or the timely introduction of a training programme will enhance the professional reputation not only of the HR practitioners directly involved, but of everyone in the function.

For example, at Ilford, part of the Imaging Products Division of the US-owned company International Paper, the contribution of HR to quality management has been recognised by its receipt (on many occasions) of the company's Internal Quality Supplier Award. The head of HR, Frank Sharp, and his team are active at many stages in quality management, from the shaping of the initiative through to the training courses, communications and involvement, management development and employee relations. The recognition they have received for their contribution to quality management has enhanced their reputation within the organisation.

Continuity

It is much more cost effective to allocate resources to building a strong brand image than it is to promote individual services or programmes, which will change over time. The brand and the values associated with it can give the HR function a 'value' that outlives the shelf life of individual programmes and initiatives.

Managing the HR brand

Effective brand management relies on a clear understanding of the value of the brand to the customer. For HR practitioners, the starting point has to be the current value clients and customers attach to the HR function. The point to recognise is that, whether they like it or not, there is already an informal HR brand defined by the culture of the organisation. In other words, people automatically attach a value to what HR does based on what they know about it from past dealings with HR and from the corporate grapevine.

At the same time, line managers and employees make assumptions about the contribution HR makes to the business from its place in the pecking order of the organisation. In particular their opinion is influenced by factors such as whether there is an HR director on the board, whether HR takes a lead on quality, and what they think of the professionalism and competence of the HR practitioners they deal with directly.

In one company in the ITEM survey, for example, line managers had nicknamed the personnel function the 'non-personnel function' because of the insensitive way it handled employees' problems. Within that organisation, that was the personnel brand.

However, by recognising the power of branding, HR practitioners can begin to shape a brand image that reinforces the position they want to have in the internal marketplace. In reality, all they are doing is creating a formal HR brand which they can begin to manage. It is important to realise, however, that the cultural assumptions which underpin the informal HR brand run deep, and that changing them takes time. In other words, to achieve more than a superficial effect, HR will have to alter the culture itself.

We discussed the importance of the internal environment to the formulation of an HR marketing plan in Chapter 1. There we made the implicit assumption that the internal environment is set, which from the perspective of where you start from it clearly is. However, a strategy to change the HR brand must look beyond the current environment to determine the prospects for altering the way HR is seen in the future. The ability of HR practitioners to change the HR brand will depend to a large extent on how receptive the culture of the organisation is to the new brand image.

115

The impact of culture on brand positioning

Organisations are built around cultural assumptions as much as they are around external market assumptions. An effective HR marketing strategy recognises that the two go hand in hand. The cultural variation from department to department can be seen in the language they use. Compare the vocabulary, for example, of data processing and HR – it is a wonder they ever understand each other.

The impact of different cultures can easily be seen from the relative status of different functions within organisations. Contrast, for instance, the culture of a high street bank with that of an advertising agency. There are no prizes for guessing which of the two will have a cultural bias towards creative functions, and which will attach greater value to the accounting side of the business. The same is true of HR; some organisations have a culture that is receptive to ideas from HR, while in others the HR function will have to overcome a strong negative bias.

It is a lot easier to build on an existing HR-friendly culture than to change to one. Research by Stanley Davies[3] in the United States suggests that, in the absence of a cataclysmic crisis, the weaker the fit of any planned change the more resistance it will meet. Of course, it is much simpler to see the effects of culture than to put your finger on exactly what it is made up of, or for that matter how to change it.

Professor Ed Schein of MIT's Sloan School of Management provides a useful analysis.[4] According to him, an organisation's culture is made up of lessons that the organisation has learned over the course of its history. Culture then, he says, is the set of basic assumptions which have worked well enough to be considered 'valid'. Typically, it will have three distinct levels.

At the behaviourial or 'artifactual' level there are the visible aspects of the organisation – its physical layout, office landscape, dress codes, slogans, noise levels and emotional climate. This is the level most apparent to outsiders. These artifacts clearly say something important about the organisation, but it is difficult to know precisely what unless you are a participant in the culture.

116

If you ask managers and employees about their visible behaviour patterns, you begin to build up a picture of the second level of culture – the values and principles on which the observed behaviour is based. So, to continue the earlier example, the culture of a bank may reflect a belief that success depends on discipline and respect for the management hierarchy. Those functions which exhibit high levels of financial discipline and have board representation will be highly regarded as a consequence. Alternatively, the culture of the advertising agency may be based on a belief that success depends on everyone thinking for themselves. In this case there will be less respect for authority and a livelier exchange of views. In both organisations, the culture will be supported by stories of past events – good and bad – that are part of the organisation's folklore and which support its values.

At the third level is the essence of the culture – the underlying assumptions from which both the behaviour and the values are derived. In the bank, for instance, this may be an implicit assumption that customers expect the management of their money to be undertaken in a serious and highly structured manner. The advertising agency, on the other hand, may assume that its customers demand a challenging and creative environment that constantly questions sacred cows.

HR practitioners seeking to effect a change in the way they are perceived by other functions – to change the HR brand – must understand the power of the existing culture to override and contradict the new message they are trying to put across. It is not enough simply to tell people that the role of the HR function has changed. The first thing they will do is test it against the old culture. So, for example, they will immediately look to see who is driving important initiatives and assume that the standing of the individuals involved reflects the importance the organisation attaches to it. If HR initiatives are seen to have the support of the main 'movers and shakers' in the organisation, then the initiative will be taken seriously, and the standing of HR will be increased. If, however, as often is the case, the initiative receives no more than lip service from senior managers and the real hands-on work is being carried out by people seen as having nothing better to do, then the old culture will inform people that nothing much has happened.

Changing culture depends on addressing the expectations that underpin it at all three levels. Yet it is rare for internal functions, or organisations as a whole come to that, to look beyond the first level.

At a macro level, companies try to match strategic decisions to the prevailing market and operational conditions. The same should be true of HR functions operating internally. Ideally, then, the chosen HR strategy should fit with the existing internal parameters defined by the organisation's culture so that the strategic objectives of the HR function are in step with the cultural mood of the business. This is not always possible of course, but an awareness of the existing culture and the knowledge that it can only be changed over time can greatly improve a strategy's chances of success.

One of the biggest problems HR professionals face in developing a strategic approach is that a great many organisations are in a state of flux, changing their market position and the culture that goes with it. But change represents an opportunity for HR functions that use marketing techniques to manage their brand image more effectively. By recognising its starting position, an HR department can tailor its marketing more effectively and affect a change in the way it is viewed in the culture of the organisation gradually over time.

The outcome of brand positioning pursued by HR functions will depend on the underlying assumptions about HR as defined by the culture of the organisation. There are three categories of culture:

- HR-friendly
- HR-neutral
- HR-hostile.

HR-friendly cultures are ones where the HR brand already has a high reputation in the organisation. Typically, HR will automatically be represented, or have access, at board level in these organisations. The reputation of the HR function in these organisations carries a strong cultural reinforcement of HR values. Their reputation helps them to acquire high-calibre staff; it develops high expectations among internal customers that are automatically reflected in staff behaviour; and it promotes word-of-mouth advertising inside the organisation.

Shepherd Construction, for example, is an HR-friendly culture. Peter Blackburn, the company's training manager, acknowledges that the culture of the company, which is highly supportive of the HR function, and the personal commitment of the senior management, were critical factors in the decision to raise the profile of HR by going for IIP recognition. And as Blackburn points out: 'It also had a very good fit with our culture and what we were trying to achieve.' The culture at Nissan, which is described later in this chapter, is another example of an HR-friendly culture.

HR functions in these organisations should use their energies to reinforce the elements that have created their reputation, defend the reputation against encroachments or misguided changes of policy and seek to maintain the size of the reputation gap.

HR-neutral cultures exist in organisations which are ambivalent towards HR. They can be transformed into HR-friendly ones by departments which have strong ambitions towards achieving an internal customer orientation and are determined to raise their profile within their organisations. Such proactive departments are typified by committed, visionary HR leaders who set challenging goals and expend a great deal of personal energy ensuring that each HR initiative receives the resources and support it needs. The head of HR is likely to have earned a place on the board, or to be influential with members of the board. In this way, he or she will raise the credibility of HR within the culture of the organisation. For example, the creation of Rover Learning Business and its establishment of a new 'learning' agenda at Rover was inspired by the leadership of the then head of HR, Rob Meakin, who subsequently gained a position on the Rover board.

Alternatively, an awareness of the strategic potential of

HR may be confined to a relatively small group of enthusiasts and practitioners. Their standing within the organisation will determine whether they are able to influence the culture. Often such organisations have implemented HR initiatives largely against their inclination. While top management pays lip service to the concept and may spend large sums of money on such initiatives, they lack the passionate belief that it is the only way forward – and hence so do all other layers of the organisation. In some cases, however, a well-conceived initiative can alter the perception of the organisation that the HR department is following the latest fad.

The Bristol and West Building Society, for example, introduced a major mentoring programme for all its managers as part of an integrated change management strategy. The team who implemented it were convinced of the benefits it would bring, but some managers were doubtful.

The team – part of the organisational development department in this instance – selected a large number of key managers in the business to be mentored by outside consultants. Regular audits were built in to assess the programme's effectiveness and to verify that real benefits were being achieved. This mechanism also provided an excellent way to demonstrate to the organisation the value of mentoring. Six months into the programme, when the managers were invited to comment on the mentoring experience, the majority reported that it had been immensely useful to them. The programme has now been developed to provide internal coaching involving line managers.

HR-hostile cultures are usually symptomatic of an HR department which in the past has had a poor reputation. Worse still, the cultural perception is often that HR initiatives are really just a tool to reduce the head-count. Just as a good reputation lingers, so does a poor one. The HR functions in these organisations are typically bedevilled by a culture that supports very different objectives, and line managers with a high level of cynicism towards any new HR initiative that requires an input from them. Customer cynicism creates a major initial barrier for any HR initiative to overcome. In most cases, a significant improvement in the cultural attitude towards the HR department in these organisations will require a drastic reinterpretation of the role of HR by senior management.

In the short term, most HR functions operating in an HR-hostile culture will be best served by simply doing what they have to in order to remain an internal support function. Over time they may be able to improve their market positioning but it will take a long time and a great deal of determination.

One final point about culture change: it is common to hear people talk about culture change as if it were somehow a discrete activity, something you buy in a packet and sprinkle around the organisation like organic manure. The reality is very different. Culture is much more like DNA: it is the genetic make-up of the organisation and needs gene therapy or major surgery to change it. Changing culture demands dramatic gestures, such as, for example, restructuring the HR department to ensure customers really are at the top of the pyramid. In extreme cases, this will take a very long time indeed, or will need a dramatic shake out of personnel staff at all levels.

The HR mission statement

A useful tool for developing the HR brand is the HR mission statement. This is a statement of general intent which creates a focus for all the function's activities. It is the vision of what the HR supplier is trying to become in the eyes of its customers and clients. An HR mission statement that articulates the function's brand values play a valuable part in aligning HR staff behind the strategy.

Many organisations now have a mission statement. The best ones articulate the vision the organisation has of itself in the future, and express genuinely held values and beliefs that all employees can align with. At the next level down, individual functions are now also beginning to recognise the value of a mission statement to inform the people inside the function and the organisation at large of their overall objectives. Here too there are good and bad mission statements. The best functional mission statements are ones that not only meet the aspirations of the individuals within the function but clearly dovetail with the mission statement of the organisation.

An HR mission statement should encapsulate the overriding objectives of the HR function, whilst at the same time supporting the mission statement of the organisation. The value of such a statement is threefold. First, it places the need to work towards a future vision of HR clearly on the HR agenda and starts the process of educating HR staff to think along the lines of achieving its objectives. In other words, it encourages HR staff to become more market-oriented and to focus their attention on what they can do to build a brand image that fits their vision for HR.

Secondly, it signals to the rest of the organisation the vision of its role to which HR aspires in the future – this in itself will cause a few raised eyebrows, which is not necessarily a bad thing – and will raise the profile of HR.

Thirdly, it provides a check against the organisational mission statement. For example, the mission statement of the personnel function at New Forest District Council is simply:

> to establish and promote the corporate image of New Forest District Council as an organisation which is highly respected for the quality and value of its services and for its reputation as a good employer.

To be effective, an HR mission statement might include the following:

- the *brand name* under which the HR function will pursue its aims, eg personnel, HR or even a title that breaks with the norm. The decision to create Rover Learning Business, for example, was inspired by the need to break with the past and present a radically different approach to training. Barrie Oxtoby, a senior training manager at RLB, came up with the name because it fused the important elements of the new entity: it was created to service the needs of the Rover Group; it represented a

shift from traditional training based on teaching to one that championed the learning aspirations of employees; and it was to be as much as possible a self-contained business unit accountable for meeting business targets.
- a *definition of the role* HR sees for itself within the organisation, ie internal consultancy, traditional personnel function, trainer etc.
- the *market segments* it aims to serve
- the *strategic objectives* HR aims to achieve
- the *types of activities* HR will engage in to achieve those objectives
- a statement of HR *brand values*.

The HR function at the American telecommunications company AT&T, for example, has the following mission statement:

> AT&T corporate education: The corporate education and training organisation supports AT&T's need to improve learning opportunities for customers and employees by delivering a wide range of programmes and courses worldwide through partnerships with all education and training groups.

That of another American company, William M. Mercer Inc, states:

> The corporate professional development group provides internal consulting services to enhance performance for individuals and groups. We do this through the application of performance interventions which enhance employee satisfaction and growth, improve efficiency, competitiveness and profitability.

Brand values

Brand values flow from the HR mission statement, which itself should flow from the business strategy. They are values that are important to HR customers and staff. Both know that the brand incorporates certain values and assumptions that they feel comfortable with. In the long run, the brand values and the values of individuals within the organisation will become synonymous, making it unthinkable to switch to another brand.

The following example shows what can be achieved using brand values to support careful market repositioning. In June 1988, Moira Holmes was appointed to head a traditional centralist personnel function at New Forest District Council. At that time, the function was largely administrative with little time or energy devoted to what she calls 'the professional role'.

'Not surprisingly,' she says, 'many managers found personnel's involvement in daily operations irksome, time-wasting and an encroachment on their ability to act.' Others, she notes, found it a comfort that they were not accountable when things went wrong.

The aim was to empower line managers to assume responsibility for the daily management of their human resource. To achieve it, she knew, a change in the culture of the personnel team was necessary. Common purpose and values were vital to achieving the commitment of the function. Personnel's simple mission statement (see p. 122) was supported by a set of values:

- Put the customer first.
- Pursue excellence.
- Create an environment of openness and trust.
- Promote a positive attitude towards change.
- Encourage competition and the will to win.
- Value initiative and participation.
- Recognise individual contributions.
- Put decision making close to the source of information.
- Develop a sense of corporate unity and achievement.

The next stage was to gain the support of the corporate management team. Gaining support for a new enabling personnel role was relatively easy because the control regime was not popular. But the management team was worried that members would not buy in to the idea of a personnel mission statement and values. Personnel opted to modify the language to market its new image. The mission was presented as its 'aim' and the values as its 'principles'. In this way it secured agreement to proceed with the programme of devolution. The daily controlling role of personnel was to be replaced by a framework of legal parameters and good practice standards. Within these there would be room for managerial discretion. It would be supported by management development, training and expert advice from the centre.

Recruitment was the first area tackled. Skills training in recruitment and selection was increased. A handbook was developed on planning and implementing recruitment. The involvement of personnel was on a consultancy basis only. As licensed psychometric testers, for instance, personnel staff were able to offer a range of assessment centre techniques. And as Holmes explains, the value of these services grew as the cost to line managers of getting it wrong became more evident.

The issue of contracts was next on the agenda. A computerised package was developed with standard contracts and statements of particulars and a range of optional variations to meet individual job requirements. A manual was produced to back up the computer programme with management guidance, and it has been commended by ACAS.

Industrial relations also became the responsibility of line managers. All employment-related proposals required early consultation with trade unions. Management advice notes, which set out the informal and formal processes, are now the cornerstone of the empowerment programme. They cover a wide range of issues from induction to political restrictions and redundancy. They set the legislative parameters and the good practice standards for human resource management, and have also been commended by ACAS.

But devolution was only part of the story. Running parallel to it was the development of a strategy for securing employee involvement, corporate belonging and ownership. Says Holmes: 'Our early initiatives in this direction raised some eyebrows. We held open days, invited managers and staff to drop in and learn more about us and make suggestions for improving our service. More than 100 people dropped in during the first event.' So successful were these open days that they sprang up elsewhere. One started in planning, another in housing. Revenue had one, which led on to customer surgeries on the community charge. Throughout the organisation, departmental barriers started to come down.

The views of all employees were sought on what the council's values should be. This has led to a set of values which are truly owned:

- caring
- openness and trust
- positive thinking
- quality
- working together
- communications
- simplicity
- value for money.

Personnel was happy to embrace the new values in place of its earlier ones. They have become the foundation of the authority's management strategy. A booklet subtitled 'How we aim to run things' is issued to all employees and underpins induction events. It calls on employees to accept personal responsibility for improving the way things are done and for ensuring that the council's values are upheld. A suggestion scheme encourages involvement.

And has the personnel function benefited from any of this? 'Yes it has,' says Moira Holmes. 'It is now represented, through directorship, on the corporate management team.' But, she adds, 'Demand for an expert consultancy service grows as the competence and confidence of managers increases. Personnel professionals' expertise needs to match that demand.'

From another perspective, HR brand values represent the essence of the HR philosophy. As Philip Ashmore, personnel manager at Nissan Motor UK (NMUK) explained it at a recent conference organised by IIR,

> Strategies are about plans to reach objectives; philosophies are about beliefs and values. The one spawns the other; philosophy is the father of a strategy.

Since Peter Wickens, UK director of personnel at NMUK, wrote *The Road to Nissan* in 1987,[5] much more has become known about what the company calls 'the Nissan way'. A key part of the company's success is the emphasis it places on managing its human resources. The personnel brand values are an essential part of the company's corporate values. Each employee is given a written statement of the company's philosophy which they can refer to throughout their working life at Nissan. This philosophy covers the main tenets, the most important aspects, of running the business at NMUK. They underline the importance of people and of team working.

An alternative set of generic values aims to promote HR as:

- useful/relevant – 'we can help you personally and in your job'
- empathetic – 'we care about you and your problems'
- capable – 'we have the professional skills to advise you'
- approachable – 'it is easy to do business with us'
- trustworthy – 'we have strong professional integrity; we are not top management's errand boys'

Delivering the brand values

Next comes the hard bit; ensuring that you live up to the mission statement and deliver the brand values. To do so, resources must be managed as competently as they are in other functions. In fact, they must be better managed.

Table 7.1 shows how brand values can be matched to HR activities to ensure that they are delivered. Some boxes have been filled in to give examples of areas in which an HR function might begin to bring its brand to life.

At British Airways, for example, the HR function has matched its own brand values and policies to the company's business plan. Chris Byron, one of BA's general managers for human resources, explains.

> Branding HR itself may or may not help build relationships with customers. It can be much more important to brand key

127

Table 7.1
Delivering the brand: an example

Brand values / Areas of activity	Strategic thinking – driven by HR	HR professionalism	Close identity with customers	Piloting best management practice	Value awareness	Innovation change management
Right people – right job	Recruitment policy Succession planning					
Motivation	Raising of HR profile	HR communications plan Peer recognition			Newsletter/in-house magazine	Raise HR profile
Commitment	Roll-out business plan		Recognition schemes			
Developing talent				Best practice training Management briefings		
Teamwork		Industrial relations				
Service excellence	Quality appraisals	Customer service contracts			Corporate recognition schemes	
Safety/social responsibility			Schools programme Involvement in the community			Social audit

initiatives. External providers will use branding to sell to your customers, and if you intend to compete, you may have to do the same.

HR policies should flow out of the business plan. Traditionally, companies say, for example, we must have a good performance appraisal system. Now we say, "what does the business plan indicate we need?" Taking this approach adds a lot to the credibility of HR by making it more business relevant'.

Calling the function HR rather than personnel symbolised a fundamental change in culture and approach; it showed HR was committed to getting closer to the business plan. Says Chris Byron: 'In the mid-1980s, BA decided that its principal driver and *raison d'être* flowed out of satisfaction amongst customers and employees; that there was an indivisible link between employee satisfaction and customer satisfaction.' Out of that commitment emerged a variety of supporting policies that related to:

- relevant training programmes
- relevant reward systems
- appropriate performance management systems.

From this analysis came decisions with top management on the skills and competencies needed to deliver the business vision. For example, the performance management system was changed to reinforce key management behaviours. So now 60 per cent of the annual bonus is based upon business results and 40 per cent on management behaviours. In addition, says Byron, 'All training courses were reviewed against the required behaviours.'

Changes in strategy now automatically stimulate changes in HR deliverables. An increasing focus by BA on globalism as a strategic issue has resulted in a review of the appropriate management behaviour and the ways in which HR can help develop those behaviours.

HR promotions

Much of what HR can do to sell the HR brand to the organisation can be described in marketing parlance as promotion. The main purpose of promotion is to improve the image and credibility of the supplier in the eyes of clients and customers.

In their book *Marketing HRD within Organisations*,[6] Jerry Gilley and Steven Eggland suggest there are two basic types of promotion:

- personal promotion through face-to-face encounters between HR practitioners and clients/customers – these can be formal, as when you use a client panel to obtain feedback, or informal, as in a chat in the canteen
- impersonal promotions, including branded media such as brochures, calenders, diaries, newsletters and articles in employee magazines.

Personal promotions are generally regarded as carrying more weight with the target audience, but impersonal promotions are useful for reaching a wider audience and for reinforcing brand values. Both sorts of promotion should be included in the HR marketing plan, although the mix will vary according to the budget and circumstances of the individual HR department concerned.

To get the right mix of promotional activities it is important to have a clear understanding of the purpose for which the promotion is to be used. There are three main purposes for which a promotion might be used:

- to inform
- to persuade
- to remind.

The first of these seeks to relay information that the target audience is probably not aware of. This could be anything from the details of a new training programme, to the venue for the Christmas party.

The second aims to alter the perception of its target audience by presenting compelling information about HR. This might include making the business case for a particular HR initiative, case studies that demonstrate what HR has achieved, or information about the future labour market from an external source.

The third will be reinforcing an earlier message. It might, for example, be used to build awareness of the HR brand by reminding the target audience about previous HR successes, or as a refresher course for line managers with personnel responsibilities, or it may even involve dropping in for a chat to remind line managers that HR is there to help if they need it.

Building a brand image for the organisation

For the purposes of this book we have concentrated on the benefits of developing an internal HR brand, but there is another dimension to the branding role that HR can play, and that is in terms of establishing the organisation as a 'good brand employer'.

In his book *Parkinson's Law*,[7] C. N. Parkinson suggested as long ago as 1960 that the perfect recruitment advertisement would be one that 'would attract only one reply and that from the right man'. But writing in the *Journal of General Management*[8] Tom Redman and Brian Mathews of the Teesside Business School, who have done a considerable amount of research in the area of recruitment advertising, point out that quite apart from the outdated notion of the right applicant being male, the credibility of the recruitment process relies on attracting a wide field of applicants from whom the best can be selected. To do so, the advertisement itself must attract attention, generate interest and stimulate action.

However, they point out that much of the literature that has been written on this subject is critical of the lack of professionalism evident in recruitment advertising practice. Estimates by the Advertising Association suggest that employers spent £650 million on newspaper advertisements alone. Individual organisations spend what might be considered extremely large sums of money to reach the right calibre of applicant. In a single year, some large companies, such as British Airways, may spend in excess of £1 million on recruitment advertising. This must, of course, be put into the context of a £40 million annual spend on corporate advertising, but the quality of recruitment advertising should clearly be a matter of concern to the HR profession.

Several organisations are now trying to achieve a synergy and coherence between corporate and recruitment advertising. Particularly prominent in this area are the award-winning advertisements of the Apple computer company and Ford. These recruitment advertisements contain a message about new products, new technologies or product performance. Accountants Price Waterhouse also use their recruitment advertisements as part of their general marketing strategy, reasoning that those executives who flick through the appointments pages are also potential users of their services. Commentators argue that sound, professional recruitment advertising can offer a variety of benefits to the organisation's product and corporate images. Writing in *Personnel Today*,[9] S. Lodge notes that many other companies are starting to follow this lead. It is safe to conclude that whatever the real benefits of such approaches, poor recruitment advertising will do nothing to enhance the organisation's wider image.

A recent TV campaign by the National Westminster Bank shows how the process can also be operated in reverse. The advertisements depict a young couple, both of whom are employees. The aim is to project to the public an image of a friendly, happy bank, but a more subtle message is embedded for school leavers in influencing their choice of employer and enhancing the bank's brand as an attractive employer. Redman and Mathews quote one HR practitioner as saying: 'I am suffering from jealousy. Why have I never worked for an organisation where the brand managers see an advantage in praising the people as well as the product? It saves so much effort in the recruitment process. I am enjoying the NatWest addictive vision of nurture, equal opportunities and careers being fun. I think the charm of those life stories will last longer than any suggestion of redundancies.'

Perhaps the time has come for HR professionals to have a quiet word with brand managers and see if they cannot get a better return on their recruitment advertising spend.

Checklist

- Does HR have a positive brand image in your organis-ation?
- Could you do more to promote the HR brand?
- Do you have an HR mission statement?
- What are your HR brand values?
- Do your HR brand values support the HR strategy and mission?
- What does HR do to articulate its brand values to internal customers? (Are they, for example, incorporated into HR communications?)
- Are the materials HR produces clearly marked so that internal customers know which department produced them?
- Could you use branding more effectively to raise the visibility of the HR function?
- Could you do more with your recruitment budget to promote your organisation as a good brand employer?

8
Communicating the Message

Most of us realise that what we communicate is what others will know about us. The difficult part for many of us to grasp in our professional lives, however, is that communication does not stop when we stop trying to put across a particular message. In fact, in most cases it is what we communicate when we are *not* trying that informs others of the 'truth' of the messages we consciously send. For example, how many of us form our opinions about what a politician really stands for simply from what they say when they are being interviewed on television or the radio? Rather, we interpret their words according to what we already 'know' about them to see whether it is consistent with what they are telling us.

The same is true, of course, of the people with whom we work. In fact, everything we do sends a message to those around us. In the case of HR, for example, even a badly organised Christmas party sends a message about the competence of the function to the organisation at large. That is why, if HR practitioners are to improve their brand image, they have to ensure that the message they send is one of competence and managerial ability in everything they do.

In the course of interviewing line managers in one company, for example, we spoke to one who complained that memos from the HR department were often riddled with spelling mistakes and inaccuracies. She went on to tell the story of an important conference organised by HR for which the letter informing line managers about the details of the event, including the itinerary, times and name of the conference suite, omitted to tell them which hotel it was to be held at. The memory of this one miscommunication had stuck in her mind and clearly influenced her view of HR competence. If this slip had been other than typical of the department, it probably would not have had the impact that it did. But in this particular case it confirmed her opinion.

We can only guess at how many other people she has repeated the story to within her organisation. It is not hard to imagine the power of such word-of-mouth advertising repeated many times.

The communications approach of the HR function

The 1991 ITEM survey[1] revealed some interesting points about how the way HR communicates with other functions affects its overall impact and effectiveness. In particular, it showed the importance of:

- *One-to-one contact* – in organisations with regular one-to-one contact between individual line managers and HR staff, there is a better working relationship between functions and a greater degree of HR integration with the business.
- *Good formal and informal communications channels* – organisations where HR is perceived as 'adding value' to the operation are typically those with good communication channels at both a structured, formal level, through scheduled meetings and presentations, and at an unstructured level through informal 'chats' to see how managers are getting on. As one line manager observed: 'In the old days the only time we heard from personnel was when there was a problem. If that's the only point of contact it colours the relationship'. The line manager concerned now speaks to HR at least three times a week and is sympathetic to HR objectives.

The survey also found that one of the most common problems for HR is its failure to communicate HR objectives effectively to line managers.

The majority of line managers interviewed said they were unclear about the overall aims of the HR function in their organisation. A number of these felt that it was because the HR function lacked defined goals and simply muddled through. The rest, and by far the majority, put it down to poor communication of HR objectives. Other comments included:

– It's important for personnel managers to come out into the field regularly, otherwise they can't speak the language of the line.

– If we were more aware of their skills and services, we'd know how they can support us in our jobs. They should be communicating with a 'this is what personnel can do for you' approach.

– I'd like to see a system that allowed me to write a suggestion to HR and know that I'd at least get a reply, even if it's only 'We tried that and it didn't work because . . .'

– Not everyone in the company actually knows what HR is really all about. The image is still very woolly. They don't need expensive videos etc, some good old-fashioned hand-shaking would probably do more in terms of reaching junior staff.

– The professional competence of the HR department is seriously hindered by a striking lack of computerisation which means they have to rely on line managers for statistical information. A while ago, the general manager wanted to know how many staff were at one of our offices, but HR didn't know and had to ask.

– The HR function doesn't promote itself enough. They should use a video to catch peoples' attention and shout their message loud and clear.

– I don't know what services HR offers.

– I find the lines of communication much better since the clarification of responsibilities.

– HR would gain support by widening the decision-making process to allow line managers to know that decisions are balanced and take business needs into account. Better communication on this one issue would raise HR credibility.

When asked what would influence their opinion of the HR function, over half of the line managers interviewed referred to improving communications as a major issue.

Improving communications

The survey shows that many HR departments have not only fallen behind in the use of sophisticated information tech-

Figure 8.1
The communications matrix

METHOD				
	Face-to-face contact	Written	Electronic	Audio-visual
Relationship building				
Information about changes in policy or services				
Problem solving				
Feedback/complaints				
Provision of regular data, eg salary scales				

MESSAGE

nology systems, but are also neglecting simple, inexpensive techniques such as staff notice boards.

The communications matrix in Figure 8.1 is designed to focus attention on the wide range of options and permutations available to get the message across. Clearly each of the communications methods shown offers a further range of detailed options. The point of the exercise is to realise that there are combinations of ways of communicating that go far beyond the traditional HR approach.

Getting the message across

The best methods of communication are often those which have a natural fit with the culture of the organisation. For example, line managers in heavy manufacturing may be unmoved by slick presentations, while those in an advertising agency may resist attempts to put a message across in what they regard as an amateurish way. The same is true of functional cultures.

Our research shows, too, that line managers attach great importance to the most simple – and inexpensive – communications methods. Regular one-to-one contact through informal chats, for example, or visits to outlying sites, are seen by line managers as valuable techniques to keep HR in touch with the sharp end of the business and to bind the organisation together.

At the other end of the communications spectrum, the need to build brand awareness and loyalty using overarching internal communications strategies is already accepted by some organisations. For example, Ford is among a handful of companies in Britain to install in-house TV networks which relay company news and relevant external developments to employees almost as they happen.

At the heart of the communications issue are some very simple questions which HR practitioners should ask both themselves and, more importantly, their internal customers. They include:

- What information do we want to provide and why?
- What information do we want to receive and why?
- What changes in perception do we want to bring about and why?
- What are the primary communications media we should use?
- What supporting media should we have available?
- How will we measure their impact?
- How can we ensure that communication is two- or three-way?

From this a communications approach can be developed which fits with the marketing strategy. Indeed, the two should marry together as one strategy. In this way, HR can communicate its effectiveness and contribution in terms that are meaningful to its target audiences.

Having analysed the information needs of internal customers, it becomes practical to look at communications channels in terms of their effectiveness in meeting those needs. Not surprisingly, the HR function in every organisation will come to different conclusions about the correct mix of media for its internal customers, as well as the nature, frequency and scope of information required.

Using all available media

Without overloading people with information they do not want, the same principle of using a wide variety of communications media, as applied to external customers, holds true for internal customers. If a message is really important and needs to be reinforced long-term, a memo or an article in the company newspaper will not be enough. The theme needs to be reinforced in as many ways as possible.

Understanding the barriers to communication

The implicit expectation of managers that employees want to be communicated with was challenged by Carl Rogers of the University of Chicago in a *Harvard Business Review* article as long ago as 1952.[2] He pointed out that just because people hear, it does not mean they are listening. On the contrary, by evaluating what is said from their perspective rather than from that of the speaker, they often dismiss the other person's arguments without understanding them. The greater the emotional content of the exchange, the less chance there is that real listening is taking place. Rogers gets to the heart of the problem when he explains that 'most people are afraid to listen because what they hear might make them change'.

Developing the listening skills of HR staff, particularly those at the front line, is therefore an essential element of effective two-way communication. IBM, for example, measured how much time people spent listening. The company then trained staff to listen better and measured the results in terms of increased productivity.

Other major barriers to communication can be categorised as arising from issues of status, resource and direction.

Status barriers occur when people become protective of information as the source of their influence within the organisation. This is the opposite of an enabling behaviour and is becoming increasingly less tolerable. None the less, in most organisations there will be people who have to be taught that information is like seed corn – the more you disseminate, the more you receive.

The most common resource barrier is time. Managers fail to keep their direct reports sufficiently informed because they are always running from one crisis to the next. Again, an educational effort is needed, to teach these managers that sharing problems and the information that goes with them is a very good way of reducing the pressure on themselves.

Directional barriers occur because people cannot see the relevance of information they receive, or information they are supposed to gather and pass on. In some cases, there is no relevance or value, simply a requirement to fill in forms for some obsolete purpose. In others, the problem is a lack of context information.

Developing a communications strategy

The use of an innovative communications approach to put across the aims, values and even the business plan of the HR function, and to support the wider aims of the business, significantly enhances line managers' perception of the HR role and its standing within the organisation. One of the most effective ways to communicate the vision the HR function has for itself is via a publicised mission statement (see Chapter 7). This not only provides an excellent communications tool to inform the rest of the organisation about the aspirations of the HR role, it also greatly improves understanding within the function and enables HR staff to align with the prescribed role of the function.

A more detailed communications strategy for HR might include the following:

- a year-long campaign which ties in HR initiatives with the business strategy as it unfolds

140

- focusing on one clear message each month using a mix of media
- regular HR briefing sessions or presentations to top management
- a programme of HR promotions and events aimed at reinforcing key messages
- effective customer feedback systems
- facilitating inter-site communication
- measuring the effectiveness of the communications channels used.

Figure 8.2 shows how a communications strategy feeds on itself to create additional benefits for the HR function. Remember, however, that an effective communications strategy is a time-consuming project, in terms both of the time taken to design it, and the time required to service it. It is also vital to establish a high degree of transparency. 'Good news only' communications that try to hide unpalatable truths quickly become discredited. Effective communication is a two-way process. It provides an efficient system of feedback, but also a forum for criticism.

At the same time, effective communications strategies can (and in some cases should) be used for a number of specific purposes. We identify four in particular which can greatly enhance the internal HR market position. These are communicating to:

- support change
- overcome geographical and cultural separation
- add value through information
- become the primary provider of internal communications.

Communicating change

By recognising the need to explain HR objectives to those affected, practitioners can go a long way towards easing the transition to new procedures and policies. Change is most threatening when:

- the reasons for it are not clearly understood

141

Figure 8.2
The communications spiral

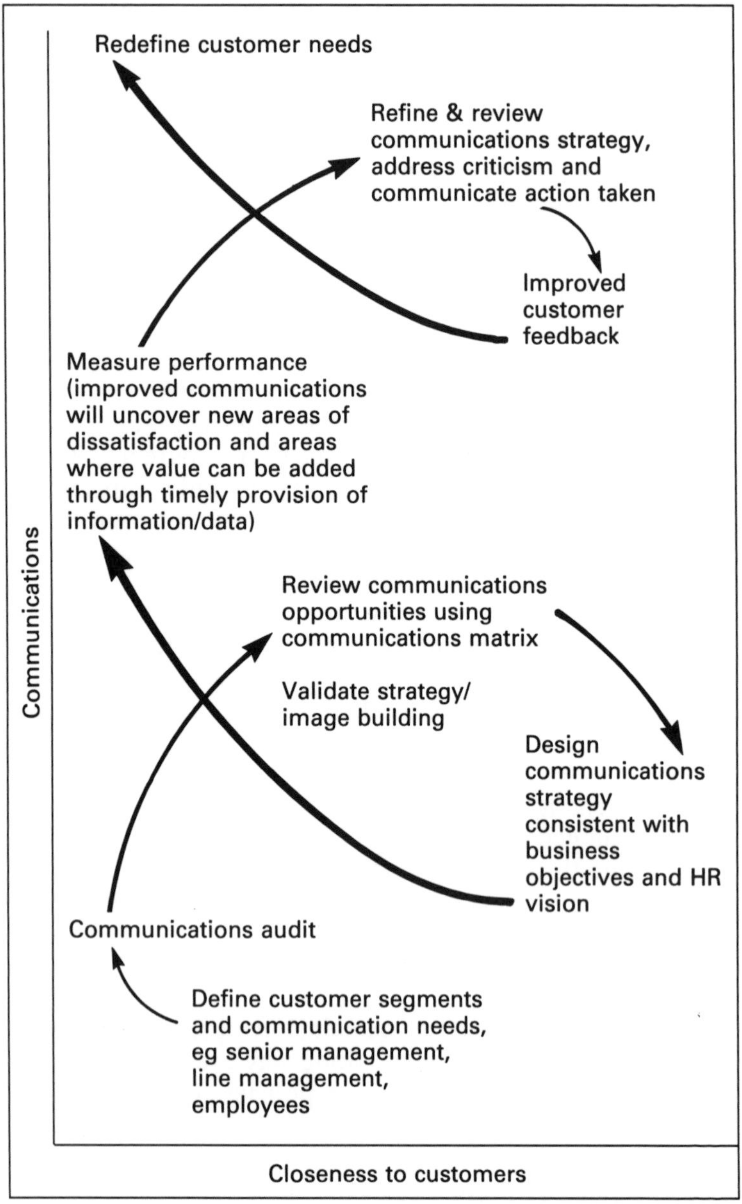

Redefine customer needs

Refine & review communications strategy, address criticism and communicate action taken

Improved customer feedback

Measure performance (improved communications will uncover new areas of dissatisfaction and areas where value can be added through timely provision of information/data)

Review communications opportunities using communications matrix

Validate strategy/ image building

Design communications strategy consistent with business objectives and HR vision

Communications audit

Define customer segments and communication needs, eg senior management, line management, employees

Communications

Closeness to customers

- it requires new behaviours or actions from those affected
- it creates new areas of responsibility for which people (usually managers) do not feel adequately prepared
- there is uncertainty resulting from poor communications or embargoed information.

Heightened communications wherever possible during such periods of change can greatly reduce resistance within the organisation. A communications strategy should be included in the implementation plan of any HR initiative and not, as is sometimes the case, as an afterthought. Communications strategies to support change are most effective when they deliver information that is:

- *Timely* – communicating early enough means that the rumour-mill does not have a chance to get started and can save a great many problems caused by the spread of disinformation. If a communication vacuum is allowed to develop, it will almost always be filled by information from the most disingenuous sources. Once rumours start they spread like wild-fire and it requires enormous effort for a fire-fighting communications initiative to put out the blaze. In the meantime, your plans may have gone up in flames.
- *Truthful* – it is a sad fact that some organisations still believe that they can pull the wool over employees' eyes. In most cases they are wrong. People have a nose for the truth and are more likely to be upset or angry if they feel they have been deceived than if they are simply told unpalatable truths. Organisations that seek to control their employees by starving them of information do both themselves and the people who work for them a grave disservice. In most situations, the truth will out sooner rather than later. It is far better to manage the way news is broken than to allow it to leak out unplanned.
- *Targeted* – the format and style should be comfortable to its intended audience. In nearly all cases, communications to support change will be different for different market segments. For instance, the presentation of information to senior managers will typically be different from that

required by line managers. So, for example, senior managers who need to digest the strategic implications of the changes, but who may not need to be informed of all the detail, might receive an executive briefing pack and a boardroom presentation. Line managers, on the other hand, may need more hand-holding communication, as they are likely to have to implement the changes with their staff. Often, too, line managers will have to brief their employees about the changes; providing them with high-quality materials to help them cascade the information adds value.

In 1991 the BP board decided to introduce a new appraisal system with several radical changes. These included moves to corporate self-appraisal and an evaluation of individuals using a set of essential behaviours, which were 'people' rather than 'job' related. The new emphasis was to be on behavioural style, not just output. At the same time, the HR function wanted to promote a process for personal development planning that would involve individuals taking personal ownership of their own career development.

The HR department in BP Chemicals recognised that to be effective the initiative would have to be owned by the line and not regarded simply as an HR requirement. HR therefore felt that a communications programme was needed to ensure that the new concepts were clearly understood by line managers and that they had the information they needed to brief their direct reports.

A communications consultancy was brought in to advise on the best way forward, and to work closely with the HR department to produce two booklets setting out the changes in a creative and easily digestible format. These booklets were distributed to all employees throughout BP Chemicals. At the same time, all managers were provided with briefing notes to help them cascade the information to staff, and attended workshops to help them learn the coaching skills they needed to work in partnership with staff in the development process.

The success of these initiatives was the result of the company's awareness that what it was trying to achieve depended on the effective communication of a variety of new concepts and a change in organisational thinking. Without a clear communications strategy to 'market' its new products, the HR department would not have secured the line ownership upon which the success of the project depended.

Communication strategies to overcome geographical and functional separation

HR departments in organisations spread between different locations have particular difficulty in co-ordinating the HR function and establishing consistent service levels. The 1991 ITEM survey shows that line managers at sites geographically removed from the centre are less inclined to consult with HR professionals, are less aware of HR objectives and have a lower perception of the contribution of the HR function than those at the centre. A significant number perceived themselves to be 'isolated' and potentially 'exposed' to HR-related problems. Moreover, experienced line managers felt that, while they themselves were well grounded in such matters, young managers away from the centre were inadequately supported by the HR department and therefore vulnerable. Comments included: 'Young managers are left to their own devices too much and are afraid to ask head office for help in case they are seen as managers who can't manage', and 'Young managers do not know what HR is there for and don't want to pester head office when they can't get a reply immediately.'

Line managers geographically removed from HR staff tended to emphasise the importance of traditional HR/ personnel roles and were less likely to perceive the benefits of a modern consultancy-based HR stance. These managers referred to poor local knowledge and a lack of understanding of their day-to-day requirements as obstacles to effective dialogue with HR. In one case, a long-standing employee was directed by the centralised HR department to act as relief staff at a site nine miles from her home despite the fact that she had no car and there was no local bus or train service. She felt, as a result, that many years of loyal service had gone unrecognised. Her line manager was equally unimpressed.

In organisations that have decentralised the HR function, geographical separation can result in inconsistency between sites. In one case, HR departments in the same organisation at different sites were perceived by line managers as 'being in competition with each other', a view supported by their insistence on the use of different forms at the two sites.

Line managers at outlying locations, or subsidiary companies, also complain that on-site HR staff, whom they see as willing to adapt, are prevented from doing so because of rigid enforcement of inappropriate HR policies from head office, or the parent company. In other words, line managers were receiving conflicting messages from local and central HR staff.

The survey showed that line managers geographically close to the HR department tended to have a clearer understanding of HR objectives and a higher perception of the value added by HR initiatives. They identified stronger lines of communication and a greater degree of informal contact with HR staff as positive influences on their perception of HR capabilities.

Other comments included:

– At present, someone could be a branch manager for ten years and never meet anyone from personnel. I'd like to see a formal consultative procedure – after all, we're the ones who work with the people in the field.

– I think HR need to be seen a lot more. We have to go to see them in their ivory tower, but they need to come out more to talk to us. I'd like to see them more proactive in this area because they would go up in everyone's estimation.

– Two years ago HR were very isolated and sat in their part of the building. They're now talking to the rest of the organisation through one-to-one meetings which are very constructive.

– I feel there is competition between the HR departments at different sites which leads to stubbornness and inefficiency. They should get their act together and be consistent.

– HR is too remote from the rest of the business at the other end of the site, which is four miles across. People at one end never see those at the other. I'd like to see HR tackle this problem for the whole organisation by making it possible for us to get together informally with other functions and begin to break down the barriers that exist.

There was widespread agreement among line managers from different organisations that regular visits, face-to-face meetings and informal telephone conversations were vital to 'put a human face on HR' wherever geographical separation was a problem.

For those who can afford it, information technology can make a valuable contribution. For example, Oxford Medical uses business TV for training at the highest and most specialised level.

Another approach, which has proved effective at British Aerospace, is to have on-site managers with a general knowledge of HR issues, who can call on specialist help from a dedicated HR resource at the centre. Figure 8.3 shows how this approach can help overcome geographical separation. For organisations with a wide geographical spread, such as retail operations and companies pursuing global business

Figure 8.3 Model to overcome geographical separation

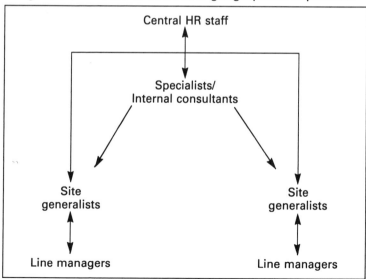

strategies, HR can add value by fostering a sense of a caring 'family'.

Some companies produce employee annual reports (EARs) to communicate financial information and business objectives to employees. A growing number of organisations recognise the considerable motivational and educational benefits that this potent form of communication offers. Thorn EMI, for example, has published an annual report for its 54,000 employees worldwide since the late 1980s. Considerable effort goes into analysing performance in the report, but Thorn also uses it as an opportunity to address other important objectives. These include the generation of a 'corporate family' feeling among a workforce that is not only scattered across the globe, but engaged in such apparently disparate tasks as promoting artistes like Tina Turner and designing infra-red tracking systems for aircraft.

Employee assistance programmes (EAPs), which provide confidential personal counselling for employees, are another way to make staff feel that the organisation cares about them; they can also pay dividends in terms of improved staff retention. According to an article in the *Financial Times* by Peggy Hollinger on 16 June 1993, 80 per cent of the top 500 US companies now run EAPs. In the UK, too, they are becoming an increasingly popular employment benefit. In the last few years some 150 UK organisations are estimated to have taken up comprehensive EAPs, including companies as diverse as Whitbread and Mobil Oil.

The counselling services are usually contracted out to specialists in the field and are often part of a wider occupational health programme. Employees, and where appropriate families, are generally given a card with a number where they can contact a counsellor either for telephone or face-to-face counselling. Problems such as depression, debt, stress, alcohol- or drug-related problems or difficulties at home can be discussed. By providing professional counselling in this way, companies can support employees whose troubles might otherwise spill over into the workplace with disastrous consequences. For example, in the case of Mobil Oil, safety is of paramount importance. Offshore workers in particular who let personal problems get in the way of their work are a safety risk not just to themselves but to their colleagues.

Communications approaches that make people at outlying sites feel 'close' can also help. For example, the use of telephone hotlines to answer questions, roadshows to explain that help is available and newsletters to keep them informed can all be effective. User panels of clients and customers can also be used as an effective way to listen to the views of those at outlying locations and to make people feel 'in touch' with the centre.

Once again, however, it is important to realise the problems associated with pursuing this sort of communications strategy over time. Maintaining a high profile in outlying sites requires adequate resourcing. Failure to live up to new expectations creates a 'flash in the pan' attitude towards HR initiatives among line managers which undermines HR credibility.

Adding value through information

Many line managers in the ITEM survey saw the provision of up-to-date information about the external job market, and the projections for future skill shortages, as the key strategic input of the HR function. They felt that their handling of HR-related issues would be improved if they had access to information about the employment market in their business sector. In some instances, the ability to provide regular job market updates, particularly of competitors' salary scales, was seen as integral to the modern HR role, and the requirement of the organisation to match its business plan with job-market trends was seen as the only justification for including HR in strategic planning. More frequently, however, this was listed as a desirable additional service that would add value to the HR function.

In organisations where line managers perceive a strong internal consultancy role for the HR function, there is also a higher expectation that HR will act as a conduit between the internal and external business environments. Moreover, HR is seen by some line managers to have a legitimate role to play in facilitating and promoting the organisation's interface with the wider community via schools, colleges, charity events and open days.

In the context of interaction with the external world, line managers in organisations with proactive HR departments said their expectations of the HR function had increased. As one young line manager put it: 'In the future we will place greater emphasis on HR to act as our eyes and ears in the external world, while we get the job done.' Acting as line managers' eyes and ears might also include providing a digest of the latest management thinking, including relevant articles, books, courses and conferences. Such a service is likely to be highly valued by busy line managers who feel they do not have time to keep abreast of developments.

Other comments included:

– I value HR as a supplier of plain facts and figures.

– I'd like hard facts about their contribution to the business. If they could show me how they have contributed to changes, I would use them more.

– I'd like to see personnel come up with positive new ideas for pay and conditions based on the specialist information they have.

– The HR director has so much information at his fingertips that would be useful to us if only we knew what he had and how it would help us.

– I want to use HR in a consultative role and as a supplier of information. I want them to be part of my management team.

– I would be impressed if HR got into the information business to service our market-research needs. It would be a good start if they did their own surveys to find out what we need. If they understood their customers better they could help us with our customers.

– I'd like more information about the training available. I've campaigned, too, for a breakdown in staff dossiers so I know what training my people have had and what that training actually involves because I'm not familiar with all the courses. Until we know what our people don't know we can't give them what they need. HR could be a great help in this.

– I'd like reports I need to arrive automatically without me having to chase them every month.

– Only some of the staff information I request arrives. I often have to dig for the rest, or make do without it.

– I would like more information on the salaries paid by our competitors. It's something that is in our internal service contract with HR, but which hasn't been delivered. I also asked for sickness statistics across the organisation for a report I was doing, but apparently they aren't available.

– We're still not getting adequate management information on wage costs which are very significant to our business. We need more information from personnel to do our jobs.

– At present we have to drag all the information we need out of the personnel department. If they shoved a lot of the administrative tasks out to other departments they could be more responsive. If information is not confidential then why lock it up when it's a legitimate business resource?

– We would benefit if HR spent more time converting theory into usable information.

– HR shouldn't wait for requests all the time. They should find out what information people want, find out the format line managers can use and give it to them. It would lead on to new services.

To be a supplier of information that adds value to line managers, HR practitioners need to be selective. Simply dumping all available data on the desks of busy line managers will do little to enhance their view of the personnel function. To add value the emphasis has to be on the provision of the right information, at the right place, in the right form. Some analysis of informational needs may be helpful in designing process solutions.

Communications structures that reflect the needs of the internal customer, as well as those of senior management, recognise that there are different types of information requiring different delivery processes. We identify three types of information:

- task-oriented
- educational or context
- motivational.

Task information　What does the employee need to know to do the job? Frequently, when employees themselves define this information, it is in very different terms from those used by managers. For example, if a company wants to encourage self-development, employees might place much greater emphasis than their managers on having additional data on existing skills levels and future requirements.

In terms of supporting cultural change, task information takes three main forms. One is the basic data about the job – its specifications and any relevant background information. The second is relevant feedback, which must be timely, accurate and presented in a way convenient for them to use. And the third relates to improvement in skills and knowledge that can be applied to the job. These elements make up pretty well everything an employee needs to have the confidence and the non-material resources to do the job.

Context information　What does the employee need to know to put his or her tasks into the broader picture? Context information can include the vision or mission statement, articles in the company newspaper about the industry sector, meetings between directors and employees to explain business strategy and so on. It is vital to ensure that people see their job as part of a larger whole. For example, Walkers Smiths Snack Foods, which is part of PepsiCo, was formed by a merger of Walkers and Smiths. Rather than impose either of the existing cultures, the decision was made to develop a new culture. To support the new culture, the HR function launched *Fresh!*, a new in-house magazine with a fresh look and lively editorial style. Upbeat stories which aimed to share best practice across the new company reinforced the openness of the new culture.

British Aerospace Military Aircraft achieved a remark-able breakthrough in context communications when it distri-buted a detailed business plan to every one of its 17,000 employees. Despite extensive editing – made necessary by commercial sensitivities and in some cases customers' security considerations – the company managed to provide a well-produced document which made a real effort to give employees a framework for decision making at a whole range of levels. Employees were able to see their own targets in the context of the business pressures facing the company. Now in its second year, the document itself is supported by an extensive briefing programme. In addition, the views of employees about the usefulness of the information provided are thoroughly researched and comments acted on.

Ford, in its new plant at Bridgend, agreed with unions to make certain business information available to employees. It is part of the company's plan to end the age-old antagonism between trade unions and management. A union representative was reported as commenting that the management/ union team at the Bridgend plant shared one objective: that the plant should prosper. Joint union and management conferences are also planned to oversee the plant business plan and product quality.

Motivational information What information does the employee need in order to feel that his or her efforts are worthwhile? Often the most difficult kind of information to pitch correctly (people tend to react negatively to being oversold), motivational information may be transmitted, for example, through relatively crude mechanisms such as incentive schemes, through stories of success and failure in the company newspaper or customised newsletters, or through verbal praise from supervisors.

Motivational information can also be used to reinforce the culture of the organisation and its values. For example, Coca-Cola & Schweppes Beverages is a very aggressive, performance-led company. The company's HR department is responsible for producing the in-house newspaper, titled *No. 1*, to reinforce business messages.

Other types of motivational information need to be fine-tuned to the needs of individuals and teams. Where it aims to foster teamwork, such information tends to work better the closer it originates to the recipient. Recognition from head office, for example, may be of less motivational impact than peer recognition and will certainly involve a much longer interval between cause and effect.

Inevitably, most of the information needed by employees will be task information, but it needs to be balanced with sufficient context and motivational information to meet both the actual and the perceived needs of the employees themselves.

However, not all the information has to be positively delivered. Active information – data supplied for a specific purpose, to stimulate specific responses – normally needs to be delivered to the employee, whether in print, verbally or electronically. Passive information – data available for purposes to be defined by the user – is usually *accessed* rather than delivered. For example, while employees may wish to know that they can review and correct their personnel files, very few will do so – the knowledge of capability is sufficiently reassuring for most people only to access the data if they have a specific issue to pursue.

Active information creates a need for the employee to know how to use it. Passive information requires a greater emphasis that the employee should know what is available and how to access it. If the employee defines a specific, recurring information need from a passive source, she or he should have the authority to change its status from passive to active (or at least the opportunity to make a case for it to be changed). The opposite may also be the case: an employee overloaded with active data may find it more useful to transfer some of that data into passive mode, to be drawn down as needed rather than automatically.

The more the individual employee or the work team can take control of defining and managing information flow, the more productive and effective they are likely to be. Key questions to be worked out with employees include:

- What decisions do I have to make, and what data do I need to make them?
- How can I put my tasks into context?
- What do I need to know to make continuous improvements?
- What information do I need to plan?
- What information do I need to assess how well I am doing against targets/standards?

- What information do I need to pass on to other people?
- What information do I need to respond to the unexpected crisis?
- What information would reinforce my confidence in myself, my colleagues and the organisation?

Based on an understanding of information need, it becomes possible to examine in detail how it is (or could best be) delivered. Key issues here are:

- Do we have the systems and resources to gather or access the information?
- Is the information available when we want it?
- Is it presented in a manner that is easy to understand and use? (Has it been designed from the point of view of the user or of the distributor?)
- What information should we be providing for our internal or external customers?

Research shows that there is a good fit here with other marketing objectives. The ITEM survey, for example, revealed that addressing internal communications needs, providing timely information in the right format and developing strategies to overcome the geographical separation of sites were among the services most valued by the 120 line managers in the sample. Where the HR department had successfully positioned itself as an effective communicator it had raised its profile and enhanced its image. And as the HR function continues to decentralise, it will become increasingly important to manage informational and communications needs.

The information employees and managers require is itself becoming ever more complex. Think, for example, of the extra data needed with the movement from collective agreements to individual contracts and performance-related pay, or in training, in measuring and evaluating competencies and implementing personal development plans. To be a worthwhile use of resources, all this information has not only to be collected from a variety of sources but shared and used across the organisation to enhance decision making on everything from recruitment to appraisal. Everyone who makes HR decisions – including a growing number of non-specialist line managers – needs to be regularly updated on key issues such as pay and employment law.

HR as a provider of internal communications

It is widely accepted now that the internal communications infrastructure is effectively the central nervous system of any organisation. There is also a growing awareness among senior managers of the impact of internal communications on the success or failure of business strategies. The corporate brain may reside in the boardroom, the analogy goes, but unless it is able to transmit messages about changes in strategy (and increasingly subtle ones at that) to the line managers who are the company's arms and legs, then it does not make a lot of difference whether you have Einstein or Humpty Dumpty making the decisions. Over time, the result will be the same – corporate paralysis, leading to a great fall.

What is not yet clear is who should own internal communications. Indeed, one of the most revealing questions to ask of top management in any organisation is: 'Who is responsible for internal communications in this company?' Most companies will have a nominal head of communications, primarily to take care of the employee newspaper and, if there is one, the employee annual report. This manager may be within the personnel department, the company secretariat, public relations, marketing or data processing, or the responsibility may be one of the many heaped upon the chief executive's secretary.

In many organisations there is a good case for HR departments to become the primary provider of internal communications. Arguments in favour include:

- HR already reaches across the functional structure of the internal organisation.
- Many HR departments have recent experience of communicating difficult messages about redundancies to employees.

- People are the function's stock-in-trade.

To do so, however, it will have to pursue proactive strategies that demonstrate competence in this area. This can best be achieved by demonstrating its ability to meet the informational and communications needs of internal clients and customers. At electrical retailers Comet, for example, the HR department was responsible for commissioning MORI to carry out a survey of employee opinions. The choice of MORI, an internationally respected research organisation, gave the exercise credibility within the organisation and gave employees the confidence to speak their minds – which after all was the stated point of the survey – in the knowledge that their replies would remain entirely anonymous.

A questionnaire was drafted and piloted through group meetings of employees to ensure that the right questions were being asked. When the survey was conducted between October and December 1992, 1,540 employees (a 32 per cent response rate – 28 per cent of staff and 50 per cent of managers) replied. The results of the survey – including criticism of management – were published as a special insert in the employee magazine.

Comet's survey overcame a common fault of internal communications; namely that it is all too often structured around management's need to give messages to employees. Very rarely does it encompass communications from employees to management or horizontally across functions. Many companies now carry out extensive attitude surveys or communications audits. But they are almost invariably too broad-brush to provide the level of understanding of communications needs required. In our experience, the results are also often distorted by other factors, such as the general motivational climate within the organisation at the time of the survey. The HR function that is really concerned to improve internal communications must accept that the issue is far too complex and deep-rooted to be dealt with by simple survey techniques. Rather, it must seek ways to empower employees by giving them perhaps the most critical authority of all – control over the information that shapes and defines what they can do within their jobs.

Checklist

- Do you have a vision for the future and an easily communicated mission statement for the HR function?
- Are HR priorities and objectives clearly communicated to line managers?
- Do line managers understand the HR role in your organisation? Has it ever been defined for them?
- How many of the following communication methods do you make use of?
  informal listening
  focus groups
  postal surveys
  telephone surveys
  formal customer visits
  open days
  complaints systems
  customer 'hotlines'
  customer advisory panels
- Do you have information at your fingertips which would be perceived as adding value to line managers?

PART IV
Making It Happen

How Much Will It Cost?

The first question many HR practitioners ask when the subject of marketing the function arises is: 'How much will it cost?' It is of course a perfectly reasonable question. The simple answer is as little or as much as they feel it is worth. But an equally valid response, at a time when every business function is striving to be regarded as a 'core' resource, might be how much will it cost *not* to market HR?

In fact, those HR departments which have taken the first tentative steps have found that internal marketing need not be expensive. The starting point is simply a commitment to asking customers – typically line managers – what HR services they value, and what can be done to improve the HR contribution. Often, marketing activities have started from a low base with something as simple as a survey of line managers' views.

For example, HR managers at Pitman Moore (one of the largest animal health companies in the world) found that a customer-satisfaction survey was a valuable starting point to transform a crisis into an opportunity. The survey provided an effective, non-confrontational basis to address HR short-comings and at the same time indicated that the HR function was willing to tackle issues proactively. It also provided a stepping stone to raising the profile of the HR function and to selling a customer-oriented HR approach to line managers.

The survey was triggered by what HR director Ian Austin describes as a 'black hole syndrome' afflicting line managers. UK managers reported that data they provided, sometimes at great pains, was being fed into Pitman Moore's European headquarters at Harefield, Uxbridge, never to see the light of day again. Although the issue did not only affect the HR function, Austin knew that to put the HR department's house in order he would have to get to the root of the matter by going directly to his customers. At the same time it was clear that if the situation was not handled sensitively there was a risk of alienating line managers still further.

Austin rejected the potentially confrontational face-to-face approach. 'Everyone knew there was a problem,' he says, 'so I didn't think it would be helpful to call line managers together just to say to them; look I'm here to be raped, so rape me.' Instead the HR department opted for the customer-satisfaction survey, which was sent out to all of the 100 or so UK managers. It was a conscious decision to treat the black hole crisis not only as a threat to HR, but also as an opportunity to create an ongoing marketing platform for the department and to provide a catalyst for a cultural repositioning of HR within the organisation.

The survey invited line managers to agree or disagree with a series of statements about the HR department. Responses took the form of a number from one to five, one indicating 'agree completely', five indicating 'disagree completely' and numbers in between showing other points on the agreement continuum. Blank spaces were also left for line managers to add their own comments.

Pitman Moore's HR managers were delighted with the 85 per cent response rate achieved by the survey. The number of completed forms, they felt, showed in itself that line managers welcomed the opportunity to voice their dissatisfaction, and the detail of their answers indicated a commitment to seeing customer-service improvements. The first step towards defusing the situation and building closer ties with internal customers had been taken.

The next step was to analyse the survey results to identify what the HR department called 'satisfaction gaps'. In fact the survey showed that, on the whole, internal customers were satisfied with most aspects of the HR role. The broad-brush picture also revealed, however, that the satisfaction gaps that did exist were linked to the *delivery* of HR products rather than the products themselves, which, by and large, were seen to meet customer requirements.

'At this point we took a hard look at the results,' says Austin, 'and we said: "This is what our customers are saying – what are we going to do?" ' The answer, the HR managers decided, was to throw the debate open to those same line managers and once again, to turn a potential threat into a marketing opportunity by involving customers in prioritising problems and shaping solutions.

As a result, line managers were invited to participate in focus groups at three different locations. They were invited to discuss an agenda raised by the survey and asked to identify 'burning issues' requiring immediate attention. The list for discussion included the following specific questions from the survey, which had had neutral or negative scores:

- The extent of training afforded by the company is adequate.
- HR encourage teamwork outside of their organisation.
- The staff in HR are commercially informed and aware.
- I feel that HR want to be part of my team and work well as such.
- HR are innovative and creative in finding solutions to problems.
- HR staff aggressively pursue issues and follow up regularly until they are completed.

Openness, Austin believes, is vital to the process. He insisted, therefore, that the survey findings and the results of the focus groups' discussions be sent out to participants in an unadulterated form. 'It is important that we air our dirty linen in public,' he says, 'and that we make commitments to our customers. We must then go back to them on a regular basis to say "this is what we said we were going to do, and this is what we've done." It is important, too, that we cascade the message down through the HR department so that we work towards total customer satisfaction'

Still on the subject of surveys, many of the line managers interviewed in the 1991 ITEM survey said that it was the first time anyone had asked their opinions on the role of HR in the organisation. In some cases, too, the decision of the HR function to participate in the survey was seen as one of the most proactive things it had ever done, and was taken as a sign that the function wanted to improve the services it provided. The cost to those HR functions taking part was simply that of taking the time to talk to a researcher.

Those still worried that marketing will automatically involve the HR function in producing costly promotional materials will be pleased to hear, too, that the survey found that most line managers are not impressed by gimmicks alone. Glossy magazines and expensive videos are not in themselves an answer. Show-biz is very rarely a substitute for substance. Both, however, can be effective tools to support an internal marketing strategy provided they are properly targeted.

Many line managers actually attach far more importance to the most simple – and inexpensive – communications methods. As we saw in Chapter 8, regular one-to-one contact through informal chats, for example, or visits to outlying sites, are seen by line managers as valuable techniques to keep HR in touch with the sharp end of the business and line managers up to date on HR matters.

Moreover, there was overwhelming support among the line managers we spoke to for the HR function to provide information about the services it had to offer. A large number said they were unclear about the current aims of the HR function in their organisation. And while several of these felt that it was because the HR function lacked defined goals and simply muddled through, the rest, and by far the majority, put it down to poor communication of HR objectives and capabilities. When asked what would raise their opinion of the HR function, over half the line managers interviewed referred to improving communication. Many of them were explicit, and comments included:

– They don't need expensive videos. Some good old-fashioned hand-shaking would probably do more to reach junior staff.

– Personnel here is like Fort Knox. I'd like to be able to just pop in and say: 'Hey I've got a problem can you, help?' But at the moment I need an appointment.

– They have got to come out of their fortress. People will not go to them any more. Around here they are referred to as the non-personnel department.

Yet the ITEM survey found that an alarming number of

personnel departments overlook the power of face-to-face contact. Worse still, they fall down on the first principles of marketing. They do not talk to line managers. And they do not listen. In several instances, for example, line managers said they had been pleasantly surprised when personnel managers actually took the time to consult them on their HR needs. One line manager from a financial services company commented: 'I was impressed when two senior personnel managers came around asking questions like: "what aren't we doing for you that you need?" '

Another point raised by the survey was that the standing of HR in the internal market is linked to the ability of its leaders to articulate the values of the function. The research shows that the personal conduct of the individual in charge sends an important signal to the organisation at large. Senior HR managers who were seen as poor communicators, or lacking interpersonal skills, were singled out as a negative influence on the overall standing of the function. This is hardly surprising when you consider that people are the HR professional's stock-in-trade. At the other end of the spectrum, HR directors held in high esteem were frequently described as 'approachable' and 'easy to talk to'. 'I've been impressed by the head of personnel,' observed one line manager. 'When he comes to see us he is always willing to jot down our ideas.'

These sorts of marketing activities certainly will not break the bank, even if they require HR prefessionals to brush up on their interpersonal skills. After all, how much does it cost to listen?

An initiative at the Department of Social Security (DSS) demonstrates, too, that part of the solution to the marketing problem lies in making more of existing opportunities. Its training arm provides training for 50,000 employees. With over 700 staff, it was – until it became an agency in its own right – the largest training department in Britain. A while ago, however, it became clear that the sheer volume of training material being generated meant that even senior training managers were unable to keep up to date with what was available in other sections of the function. An internal marketing exercise was badly needed.

For an organisation spanning over 30 separate locations the sort of roadshow approach favoured by some other HR departments was impractical. But an opportunity did exist when delegates from all the training sites came together for their annual conference. An exhibition of training products was targeted at this captive audience, with senior training managers invited to display their wares.

But it did not end there. David Jones, head of training at that time, explains. 'From talking to our managers we already knew that there was so much paper passing across their desks that they didn't have time to read it all. Then we started thinking that if our own people weren't aware of what was available, line managers probably weren't either. We realised that by inviting senior line managers to the event we could widen the marketing exercise to spread the word to other parts of the organisation as well.'

Creative approaches of this kind can go a long way towards overcoming the image problem. But there are some very simple questions all HR professionals can ask themselves and, more importantly, ask their internal clients as a first step to developing a marketing strategy. They include:

- What services do we want to provide and why?
- What information do we want to receive and why?
- What changes in perception do we want to bring about and why?
- What are the primary communication and marketing tools we should use?
- How should we support our marketing effort – ie what service guarantees should we make?
- How will we measure their impact?

It is true that answering such questions – if they are to yield worthwhile answers – will require some soul-searching on the part of HR practitioners, but in hard cash terms they do not require a large investment.

Those answers should form the basis of an HR marketing strategy. From that strategy a plan can be created with sufficient flexibility to take account of the needs of different market segments. How much money will be needed to bring that marketing plan alive really depends on the marketing methods employed. But throughout this book we have tried to indicate that it is not how much you spend, but how well you spend it that will make marketing HR a success or a failure.

It is important, too, that the marketing plan – whatever form it takes – should have clear schedules, budgets, measurements and review dates as well as clearly assigned accountability. After all, the point of the exercise is to demonstrate both the level of specialist expertise within HR and its managerial competence. By applying recognised project management systems to the implementation of the marketing plan, the function can show its effectiveness and contribution in terms that are meaningful to line managers. It is an approach which, if well executed, will dramatically improve the image of HR both with line managers and in the boardroom.

Checklist

- Do you have a clear, practical plan and budget for marketing HR?
- Can you afford *not* to market HR?

Getting Started

So what might an HR marketing plan set out to achieve? The answer will very much depend on the circumstances of the particular HR function. What struck us most from interviewing line managers and HR practitioners across a wide range of organisations was the diversity of challenges currently facing HR functions in the UK. These included: the threat from compulsory competitive tendering in public sector organisations; rigid HR policies imposed from an overseas parent company that were wholly inappropriate to the UK context; and recently privatised, or soon to be privatised, organisations where the HR function is having to radically redefine itself in a radically changed environment. In some organisations we found that effective marketing has already made important inroads into the HR image problem, while in others there was no image problem to begin with. In others again, the HR function had gone backwards in the past few years by mishandling important situations.

Such diverse circumstances make it difficult to make general prescriptions about where to start. The following cross-section of real case studies taken from the original 1991 ITEM survey highlight some of those challenges. Where possible we have tried to indicate areas where marketing could help the HR function add value.

Company A: a public sector agency

Through its competent handling of a period of rapid change and its willingness to innovate, the HR function had gained credibility with line managers and was well thought of within the organisation. Comments included: 'I have nothing but praise for the HR department', and 'Because I have not failed at an industrial tribunal yet, I am convinced that the information they give me is of a very high standard'.

HR staff were praised for their professionalism, although

availability was identified as a problem. A help desk to deal with urgent queries was suggested as a way around this difficulty. Line managers also expressed concern that response times could be improved, and that HR's understanding of their business priorities would benefit from a more structured dialogue. A striking feature of this organisation in relation to some others surveyed was the willingness demonstrated by line managers to work with the HR function towards fostering a closer relationship.

More than one line manager specifically identified internal marketing of HR services as an area requiring improvement particularly in the context of compulsory competitive tendering. Said one: 'My number one criticism is that they need to market themselves. They need to list what's on offer; tell people how good they are; tell them how much things cost; and use marketing to position themselves in the organisation.' Another said: 'Marketing will be essential in the not too distant future to meet the changing face of local government. HR will need to convince me of their efficiency and cost effectiveness. It's something we'll all be doing in three years' time, but a smart HR department will do it now to be ahead.'

Conclusions

The survey results suggest that:

- line-manager perception of HR competence is high
- communication is generally good
- the cultural attitude towards HR is positive.

These factors suggest that the environment in which the HR function operates is receptive to HR marketing initiatives.

Recommendations

The introduction of compulsory competitive tendering in the next few years represents an external threat to the HR function. HR should react by actively marketing performance gains achieved in the last few years to the rest of the organisation. HR could also use market research techniques to identify added-value services which would give it competitive advantage.

Marketing tools suggested by line managers included:

- brochures
- presentations
- a help desk.

Company B: an IT supplier

The survey showed that, by and large, line managers saw the HR function as policy- and procedures-driven. As a result the function was perceived as inflexible in its approach to individual problems, preferring to let the line cope with new situations that arose, as one line manager put it. Continuity was identified as an obstacle to closer relations between HR and the line, with line managers claiming that the HR staff they dealt with changed too frequently to form strong working relationships.

Overall, HR professionals were perceived as competent in terms of the policies, procedures and systems that were already in place, but were criticised for failing to be proactive. Some younger HR staff were seen as enthusiastic, but constrained by the culture of the function which was believed by line managers to be hostile to innovation. They also identified a head-office perspective prevalent among HR staff which made them somewhat naive in their approach to real-life situations. While they acknowledged the specialist nature of HR staff, the line managers interviewed felt that understanding would be enhanced by a greater awareness of the day-to-day responsibilities of line management.

Conclusions

Although more research would be necessary to ascertain the extent of the problem, based on this very small sample line manager confidence in the HR function appears to be at a low ebb, with line managers:

- unclear about HR objectives
- critical of what is seen as a repressive HR culture
- unaware of ways in which the HR function could add value to the organisation.

Recommendations

The survey indicates the following:

- Improving the HR response time would be a good starting point for raising the credibility of the function among line managers.
- A less rigid approach would make line managers more inclined to bring personnel problems to the HR function.
- By communicating what to begin with would probably be small HR successes, the function would gain credibility and line-manager support, enabling it to become more proactive and better placed to drive HR initiatives in the future.

Company C: a traditional heavy-industry supplier

The survey showed that, by and large, line managers were aware of the difficulties facing the HR function. They perceived that the HR department was constrained by the culture of the organisation and a lack of opportunities for enhancing the HR role due to the attitudes of line managers towards the function. Nevertheless, line managers placed a high premium on improving the speed of HR's response to queries and felt that some line managers, particularly those lacking experience of personnel issues, were vulnerable because of inadequate support from the centralised personnel department.

While nearly all line managers interviewed were sympathetic to the low level of staffing in HR (there were only two personnel specialists covering a geographically dispersed organisation) they said that they would like to see more day-to-day contact, with personnel staff making more on-site calls to ensure that problems were both identified early and dealt with thoroughly. It was also felt that greater contact at the 'sharp end' of the business would educate HR staff in the more practical needs of the line and add value to HR initiatives and problem solving.

Some line managers expressed concerns about the interpersonal aspects of the role currently played by the HR function. They felt that a more sensitive handling of employee relations would benefit the organisation as a whole. It was also suggested that the image of the HR function was tied too tightly to the model of the US parent company and would gain from moves to present a 'British face' to employees in the UK. Training, too, was felt to be inadequate and to require attention, although some line managers said that they knew it was a priority of the personnel director.

Conclusions

Line managers' comments revealed the following obstacles facing the HR function:

- inadequate resourcing in terms of HR staffing levels
- a company culture that is slow to recognise HR benefits
- a geographically scattered organisation
- inconsistent perceptions of HR responsibilities across the organisation with a need for the HR function to define itself and communicate more effectively with line managers
- poor clerical support with spelling mistakes and errors in memos etc, which detracts from the perceived competence of the HR function.

Recommendations

Little is likely to be achieved through HR marketing initiatives until the underlying cultural attitude towards HR improves. The survey results suggest that response time and providing adequate support for geographically remote line managers are critical performance criteria which could be addressed to improve HR credibility within the organisation. It seems likely, however, that additional resourcing will be required for personnel initiatives to be successful.

Company D: a financial services company

The HR function was perceived by line managers within the organisation to have improved greatly in the past couple of years, although there remained considerable scope for further improvement. HR professionals were seen as competent, with younger staff characterised as enthusiastic although lacking in experience. But line managers suggested that there were also some remnants of an old guard, who had drifted into the HR function without a specialist background and who were less helpful.

Overall, HR was seen as trying hard to address its shortcomings and making strides towards a change in the company's culture to allow it to become increasingly proactive within the organisation as a whole. There remained, however, some doubt about the implementation of ambitious HR initiatives. The profile of the department had certainly been raised in the past three years, but credibility in the eyes of line managers had yet to be established. As one line manager put it: 'There is a desire to do things well, but it often falls short of the mark because of the inexperience of the younger staff. Annoying things happen, like hearing last thing on a Friday about a new starter coming in on the following Monday.'

Specific criticisms were directed at:

- administrative processes, where the lack of computerisation was seen by line managers to detract from HR professionalism through inaccuracy and unreliability
- a movement away from the welfare role of the traditional personnel function, which had left a vacuum that line managers felt they were obliged to fill

173

- the need to concentrate on managing the day-to-day running of the function instead of spending time on high-profile HR initiatives.

On the positive side, line managers welcomed the recent introduction of an HR customer service contract which was seen as a commitment by the HR function to high levels of service and an effective marketing tool. As we have seen, however, HR credibility was not yet sufficiently solid to convince line managers that the desired gains would materialise. Those interviewed, while hopeful, were reserving judgement while they waited to see whether the programme worked in practice.

A number of line managers also perceived a continuing obstacle to rapid progress to be the culture of the parent company, which they believed tied the hands of the HR function in some areas. There was a feeling, too, that pressure from head office may sometimes be used as a convenient excuse for not getting things done.

Conclusion

There is an underlying optimism among line managers that progress made by the HR function will continue. Successful implementation of HR initiatives will boost HR credibility and position the function well for a more proactive role in the future. The HR director, in particular, is perceived to be a powerful force with the potential to initiate as well as react to change. The concerns indicated below, however, represent issues that need to be addressed in order to win the confidence of line managers and to ensure their continuing support.

Recommendations

The survey indicated that line managers would like to see:

- more information available on competitors' salary structures

- better access to professional counselling which already exists but is spread too thinly within the organisation
- bulletins explaining HR priorities
- updates on HR policy concerning salary scales, recruitment, disciplinary procedures and legal requirements
- better access to staff records
- rules and regulations interpreted to fit the circumstances instead of the other way round
- more solutions from HR instead of problems
- more personal contact with HR staff (seen to provide effective dialogue and a way to market HR's added-value services)
- the HR customer-service contract fulfilled (the customer promise kept).

If the research team, as outsiders, were able to gain such insights through a little market research in the form of a survey, what might HR departments themselves achieve through a concerted marketing effort? In the case of Wessex Water, for example, personnel found itself 'caught up in the survival game', according to the head of personnel services, David Cooper. Although his department was heavily involved in the rationalisation programme that followed the company's flotation in December 1989 and its stock-market listing in January 1990, Cooper quickly realised that, in the new environment, the personnel department's own future looked far from certain.

The move to the private sector meant that, for the first time, he and his HR colleagues had to justify the department's existence. 'We had to demonstrate our worth to the business,' says Cooper, 'and it has meant marketing our services to the organisation on the basis of HR impact on the bottom line.'

Prior to privatisation, personnel was a well-established function at the then Wessex Water Authority and operated within a national framework laid down for the water industry as part of the public sector. The changeover to a private company brought with it a radical review of the company's operations, including a fresh look at the role of the personnel function. The privatisation process itself raised the profile of the department and put the personnel issue high on the managing director's list of priorities.

In January 1991, consultants were brought in from outside the company to review the personnel function on a service-by-service basis. The aim was to devolve responsibility for employees away from the personnel department to line managers who, in keeping with the managing director's vision, were to be made more accountable for staff performance. It was decided that the role of personnel should become more support-oriented, offering specialised help with the implementation of a performance-related pay scheme and HR policies geared to improving profitability.

As a result, David Cooper, encouraged by his director, was faced with the task of changing the image and emphasis of the department from one formerly epitomised by the 'you can't do that because of our personnel policy' approach, to one that says: 'This is how we can help you achieve your goals.' Says Cooper: 'If we were to be effective in our new role we had to get away from the attitude that some managers had that they only ever came into contact with personnel when someone was hired, promoted or left the company. We'd always been seen as on the lower decks, but now we had to show that we were attached to the engine room.'

Consultation with senior management identified the following HR changes as critical to the future of the business:

- Performance-related pay, to be introduced in April 1992
- Disciplinary procedures
- Dealing with poor employee performance
- Reorganisation and rationalisation
- Absenteeism
- Selection and interviewing techniques
- Identifying potential, and linking training and development to business needs.

The problem was how to communicate the changes to senior managers and at the same time use the exercise as a marketing tool to sell the merits of the new-look personnel function. The solution, Wessex's personnel team decided, was a manual titled '*Management Guidelines*', which laid down personnel policies and procedures translated into best practice and which could be supplemented as the need arose. In addition, a personnel roadshow called 'Senior Management Update' was planned to bring the important issues to the attention of the top 200 managers.

In September 1991, the 'Senior Management Update' went on the road with each of ten stops hosted by one of Wessex's directors. 'The message we wanted to put across', says Cooper, 'is that it's the managers' job to manage, and the role of personnel to support. By getting company directors to send out the invitations, we not only encouraged managers to attend, but also ensured lively interactive discussions which led to presentations scheduled for two hours lasting as long as six.'

According to Mervyn Brown, sewage treatment manager at Wessex, the roadshow was well timed to meet the cultural changes the organisation is going through. Brown, who is responsible for a staff of 350, says: 'The roadshow was effective as a marketing tool because it was pitched at the right time to meet our needs, it was the right duration – half a day instead of a whole day – and it had the right content. As a result my managers came away with a very positive attitude towards the new personnel role.'

David Cooper is pleased with the way the roadshow has been received by senior managers and intends to hold supplementary presentations two or three times a year. He also plans to use the same marketing technique to communicate the change in culture to middle managers and below. For the personnel department, the pilot roadshow was a learning experience with the following lessons:

- Although it was called an 'update', senior managers actually knew less than personnel managers thought about the HR responsibilities they were taking on.
- The presentations tried to cover too many big issues in one roadshow with the result that they overran.
- The water industry has traditionally been a technical/task-oriented business, but marketing to senior managers drew

their attention to the people side of the business which is good for personnel in the future.

Conclusion: building long-term partnerships that work

In this book we have tried to bring together a variety of practical examples of how the human resources function can increase its value to the organisation, its influence on mainstream events, policies and strategies, and its capacity to survive amidst rapid organisational change.

Clearly, the starting point for any HR department is a willingness to listen to customers in an open, non-defensive, enquiring and active manner. Only by accepting and recognising the power of customer perceptions will HR be able to deliver at the level which will be necessary in the flatter, entrepreneurial organisations of the next decade.

Effective HR functions are increasingly learning that, just as there is no such thing as a unified customer in the external market, so the internal market is composed of different customer segments. Each of these needs to be listened to, understood and have its needs accommodated. Active listening of this kind is a continuous process and will involve a mixture of one-on-one discussions and market research techniques, neither is adequate on its own.

Having listened, HR needs to react by developing products and services that match both the day-to-day and, where appropriate, the strategic requirements of each internal customer segment. But simply responding is not enough. An increasing amount of HR activity will have to go into both educating customers to understand what they could have and how to make best use of it, and into identifying and developing proactive approaches to longer-term and future problems.

For the typical HR department, making this happen will require two fundamental changes. First, the department will have to learn how to operate in partnership mode – in essence, senior management and other key decision-makers in the organisation must be regarded as key accounts and treated accordingly. Second, HR must re-make its repu-tation. Achieving this goal will happen partly through improving the quality of delivery, raising professional standards (especially applying principles of management excellence to the HR function itself), and an intelligent and coherent approach to communicating with each internal customer segment. The words marketing and branding do not at first sight sit easily with HR, but in practice HR has to change its positioning within the internal market and these are vital tools.

No one says this will be easy. In effect, it involves a cultural revolution as dramatic as the transformation of the organisation itself. Indeed, in our opinion this cultural revolution has to happen within HR as a precursor to genuine, effective and durable cultural transformation within the organisation as a whole.

Failure by the HR department to meet this challenge will ultimately affect its chances of survival or at best consign it to marginal activity with the real influence on the organis-ation's future lying elsewhere. But those HR departments that grasp the nettle will create increasing opportunities to enhance their reputation internally and externally and to demonstrate significant benefits to the bottom line. In doing so, they will raise their profile and earn both the right to have a hand on the strategic rudder of the organisation and to survive and prosper. What more could they ask for?

APPENDICES

Appendix I The Survey

Objectives

The general objective of the exploratory study was to provide an overview in a small number of organisations of the expectations and perceived needs for personnel services among selected line and senior managers. More specific objectives included:

- establishing line managers' expectations of the operational contribution and support of the HR function and service
- reviewing line managers' perceptions of the current performance of the HR function as an internal supplier
- assessing line managers' perceptions of what this service level should be and the implications for the organisation of the HR function and for marketing the function more effectively
- examining the views and experience of personnel practitioners on these issues and on the likely barriers to achieving more effective marketing of the function to meet strategic needs.

Where practicable, a range of experience and opinion was sought within participating organisations.

Method

The report was based on the the following sources:

- survey data
- literature search
- case-study material
- comments from HR practitioners.

A telephone survey was conducted in 20 large to medium-sized organisations selected by the ITEM Group in consultation with the IPM. Selection criteria aimed to achieve a wide spread across sectors and a diversity of HR approach. In each of the participating organisations ITEM conducted interviews with between four and eight line managers from middle and senior management. The head of personnel was also interviewed and, where appropriate, other senior HR professionals within the department.

The survey questions were designed to investigate how and to what extent HR professionals are marketing the HR function within their organisations. To achieve this questions were set in the context of line managers' expectations and perceptions to identify:

- line managers' perceptions of current performance of HR as an internal supplier
- line managers' perceptions of what the service level should be
- line managers' thoughts on what the key issues are, and on what HR should do to market itself more effectively
- the personnel/ HR perception of the same issues.

The survey is reproduced in full in Appendix II.

The literature search was carried out by the IPM and ITEM to identify relevant ideas and marketing techniques.

A number of detailed case studies were collected from UK organisations where marketing techniques have been applied by the HR function. These are documented in a separate publication which accompanies the report. Finally, comments were invited from HR practitioners at the 1991 IPM Conference held in Harrogate.

Appendix II   Questions for the IPM Survey 'Marketing the HR Function'

Ask the interviewees to score each answer on a scale of 0–5 and then discuss the issue.

Line managers' questions

1. Comment on each of the following regarding the Human Resource function in your company:

- professional competence
- understanding of business priorities
- relevance of training
- service quality
- willingness/ability to adapt
- being at the leading edge
- creativity
- a major force for change within the organisation.

2. On a scale of 0–5, to what extent do you believe these things are provided?

3. What is the negative/positive impact on your own job of the way that the HR function meets these objectives?

4. What things do you think you ought to be getting from the HR function?

5. Should line managers be more precise in specifying their requirements to the HR function? How do you think you can do this?

6. Do you think HR should market itself to you? If so, in what manner?

7. What would influence your opinion of HR and why?

8. What do you really want from the HR function in terms of the product, services, and the manner in which it is delivered?

9. Do you think that HR should be involved in business planning? If so, how, at what level, and at which stage?

Human resource directors' questions

1. How do you believe line managers rate your department on:

– professional competence
– understanding of business priorities
– relevance of training
– service quality
– willingness/ability to adapt
– being at the leading edge
– creativity
– being a major force for change within the organisation?

On a scale of 0–5 what do you think you would be? On a scale of 0–5 what do you think line managers think the reality is?

2. To what extent and in what manner do you consider line-manager perceptions of the HR function affect your ability to meet:

– business objectives
– HR objectives?

3. To what extent and in what manner do you consider line-management perception of HR affects your ability to participate in setting business objectives? How does it affect your ability to participate in strategies?

4. To what extent do you believe business decisions would be improved if line managers consulted HR earlier than they normally do?

5. Do you perceive that there is a strong need for HR departments in general to market themselves?

6. What encouragement do you receive to market HR from:

– top management
– line management peers
– colleagues in the HR function?

7. Do you have a marketing plan for HR?

8. Do you carry out market research to identify line managers' actual/potential requirements?

9. What do you actually do to market yourself?

– newsletter
– internal/external advertising
– workshops
– conferences

10. What do you perceive would be the real value of marketing the HR function to:

– you
– the HR department
– the organisation as a whole?

Appendix III   New Forest District Council

Service Level Agreement Questionnaire

The purpose of this questionnaire is to obtain your views about the current level of service you receive from Personnel Services and to help us gain a clearer idea of how you might use us in the future.

If there are any points which require further clarification, please contact us on Extension 5496 at Appletree Court, Lyndhurst.

Instructions

The descriptions listed below indicate the categories of services contained within our Service Level Agreement (a copy is attached for reference).

For each description, please tick one box in each category
(a) current standards
(b) likely future demand.

Please add any additional comments in the space provided or on a separate sheet.

Description
1 **Organisational Planning, Structures and Job Grading**

Comments

Category

(a) **Current standards**
[ ] Good
[ ] Could be better
[ ] Don't know

(b) **Likely future demand**
[ ] More
[ ] Less
[ ] Same

2 **Recruitment and
Appointment**

Comments

(a) **Current standards**
[ ] Good
[ ] Could be better
[ ] Don't know

(b) **Likely future demand**
[ ] More
[ ] Less
[ ] Same

3 **Management Development
and Training**

Comments

(a) **Current standards**
[ ] Good
[ ] Could be better
[ ] Don't know

(b) **Likely future demand**
[ ] More
[ ] Less
[ ] Same

4 **Industrial Relations**

Comments

(a) **Current standards**
[ ] Good
[ ] Could be better
[ ] Don't know

(b) **Likely future demand**
[ ] More
[ ] Less
[ ] Same

5 **Health, Safety and Welfare**

Comments

(a) **Current standards**
[ ] Good
[ ] Could be better
[ ] Don't know

(b) **Likely future demand**
[ ] More
[ ] Less
[ ] Same

6 Performance Review Systems

Comments

(a) **Current standards**
[ ] Good
[ ] Could be better
[ ] Don't know

(b) **Likely future demand**
[ ] More
[ ] Less
[ ] Same

7 Pay and Conditions of Service

Comments

(a) **Current standards**
[ ] Good
[ ] Could be better
[ ] Don't know

(b) **Likely future demand**
[ ] More
[ ] Less
[ ] Same

8 Terminations

Comments

(a) **Current standards**
[ ] Good
[ ] Could be better
[ ] Don't know

(b) **Likely future demand**
[ ] More
[ ] Less
[ ] Same

9 Discipline/Grievance

Comments

(a) **Current standards**
[ ] Good
[ ] Could be better
[ ] Don't know

(b) **Likely future demand**
[ ] More
[ ] Less
[ ] Same

10 **Youth Training/Work Experience**

Comments

(a) **Current standards**
[ ] Good
[ ] Could be better
[ ] Don't know

(b) **Likely future demand**
[ ] More
[ ] Less
[ ] Same

Any further comments

Thank you for completing this questionnaire, please return it to Helen Lake, Personnel Services, Appletree Court, Lyndhurst by **20 February 1993**.

191

References for Raising the Profile of HR

Introduction:

1. *Marketing the Human Resource Function: Towards a customer-supplier relationship*. Report of the findings of a survey among line managers and HR practitioners by the ITEM Research Unit, The ITEM Group, 1991.

Chapter 1:

1. *Marketing the Human Resource Function: Towards a customer-supplier relationship*. Report of the findings of a survey among line managers and HR practitioners by the ITEM Research Unit, The ITEM Group, 1991.
2. Theodore LEVITT, 'Marketing Myopia'. *Harvard Business Review*, July–August 1960.
3. Magnus SÖDERSTRÖM, 'An HRM role struggling for survival'. *Personnel Management*, June 1993, Vol 25 No 6.
4. Nigel PIERCY and Neil MORGAN, 'Making marketing strategies work in the real world'. *Marketing Business*, Feb 1990.

Chapter 2:

1. 'The changing role of personnel', MORI, 1992.
2. 'Attitudes to personnel', MORI, 1992.
3. Susan WALKER, *Human Resources* Magazine, Summer 1992.
4. *Marketing the Human Resource Function: Towards a customer-supplier relationship*. Report of the findings of a survey among line managers and HR practitioners by the ITEM Research Unit, The ITEM Group, 1991.
5. Tom PETERS, *Thriving on Chaos*. Guild Publishing, London, 1987.
6. Index of Customer Dissatisfaction, developed by The ITEM Group, Burnham House, High Street, Burnham, Bucks SL1 7JZ.
7. Ron ZEMKE and Chip BELL, *Managing the Delivery of First Class Service*. Paper presented to the Manchester Business School to accompany workshop on service quality, Jaunary 1992.

8. David CLUTTERBUCK and Sue KERNAGHAN, *Making Customers Count: A guide to excellence in customer care*. Mercury Business Books, 1991.

Chapter 3:

1. *Training in Britain*. Department of Employment, 1989.
2. David CLUTTERBUCK and Bernard WYNNE, 'Using Evaluation Techniques'. *Gower Handbook of Training and Development*, ed. by John PRIOR MBE. Gower in association with the Institute of Training and Development, 1991.
3. David GOODHART, 'Power to personnel people', *Financial Times*, 17 June 1992.
4. Ron ZEMKE and Chip BELL, *Managing the Delivery of First Class Service*. Paper presented to the Manchester Business School to accompany workshop on service quality, January 1992.
5. BERRY, PARASURAMAN and ZEITHAML, 'Quality Counts in Services too'. *Business Horizons*, May–June 1985, Vol 28.
6. Theodore LEVITT, *The Marketing Imagination*. The Free Press, 1983.
7. ZEMKE and BELL, *Op. cit.*

Chapter 4:

1. Pauline CROFTS, 'Earning a place on the board'. *Personnel Management*, April 1993, Vol 25 No 4.
2. *Marketing the Human Resource Function: Towards a customer-supplier relationship*. Report of the findings of a survey among line managers and HR practitioners by the ITEM Research Unit, The ITEM Group, 1991.

Chapter 5:

1. INSTITUTE of PERSONNEL MANAGEMENT, *Quality: People management matters*. IPM, 1993.
2. Mick MARCHINGTON, Adrian WILKINSON and Barrie DALE, 'Who is really taking the lead on Quality?'. *Personnel Management*, April 1993, Vol 25 No 4.

Chapter 6:

1. Carl R. Rogers, *Client-Centred Therapy*. Houghton Mifflin, 1951.
2. *Marketing the Human Resource Function: Towards a customer-supplier relationship*. Report of the findings of a survey among line managers and HR practitioners by the ITEM Research Unit, The ITEM Group, 1991.
3. Regis McKenna, *Relationship Marketing: Own the market through strategic customer relationships*. Century Business, 1992.
4. *ibid*.
5. *The Human Resource Management Yearbook, 1993*, AP Information Services.

Chapter 7:

1. Philip Kotler, *Marketing Management*. Prentice-Hall, 1991.
2. *Marketing the Human Resource Function: Towards a customer-supplier relationship*. Report of the findings of a survey among line managers and HR practitioners by the ITEM Research Unit, The ITEM Group, 1991.
3. Stanley Davis, *Managing Corporate Culture*. Harper Row, New York, 1984.
4. Professor Ed Schein, 'Corporate Culture: Constraint or opportunity for strategy'. *Issues: The PA Journal for Management*, Vol 1 No 1, 1984.
5. Peter Wickins, *The Road to Nissan: Flexibility, Quality, Teamwork*. Macmillan, 1987.
6. Jerry W. Gilley and Steven A. Eggland, *Marketing HRD within Organisations*. Macmillan International Publishing Group, New York, 1992.
7. C.N. Parkinson, *Parkinson's Law: In Pursuit of Progress*. Penguin, Harmondsworth, 1960.
8. Tom Redman and Brian P. Matthews, 'Advertising for Effective Managerial Recruitment'. *Journal of General Management*, Winter 1992, Vol 18, No 2.
9. S. Lodge, 'Image Maker'. *Personal Today*, 12 June 1990, pages 25–6.

Chapter 8:

1. *Marketing the Human Resource Function: Towards a customer-supplier relationship*. Report of the findings of a survey among

line managers and HR practitioners by the ITEM Research Unit, The ITEM Group, 1991.
2. Carl R. ROGERS and F. J. ROETHLISBERGER, 'Barriers and Gateways to Communication'. *Harvard Business Review*, July–August 1952, (Reprinted HBR Nov–Dec 1991).

Bibliography and further reading

David CLUTTERBUCK and Sue KERNAGHAN. *Making Customers Count: A guide to excellence in customer care*. Mercury Business Books, 1991.

Jerry W. GILLEY and Steven A. EGGLAND. *Marketing HRD within Organisations*. Macmillan International Publishing Group, New York, 1992.

Regis McKENNA. *Relationship Marketing: Own the market through strategic customer relationships*. Century Business, 1992.

Ron ZEMKE and Chip BELL. *Managing the Delivery of First Class Service*. Paper presented to the Manchester Business School to accompany workshop on service quality, January 1992.

David CLUTTERBUCK and Bernard WYNNE. *The Service Dimension*. The ITEM Group in association with Henley Management College, 1991.

Michael J. BAKER (ed.). *The Marketing Book*. Published by Heinemann on behalf of the Institute of Marketing, 1987.

Richard R. BROOKES. *The New Marketing*. Gower, 1990.

Malcolm H. B. McDONALD. *Marketing Plans: How to prepare them: How to use them*. Second edition, Heineman Business, 1989.

John M. MURPHY (ed.). *Branding: A Key Marketing Tool*. Second edition, Macmillan, 1992.

Gerard EARLS and Patrick FORSYTH. *Making Marketing Work*. Kogan Page, 1989.

Theodore LEVITT. *The Marketing Inspiration*. The Free Press, 1983.

Index